In the Shade

In the Shade of the Sycamore Tree

Ministers Reflect on the Subject of Wealth

EDITED BY
J. Robert Moon

In the Shade of the Sycamore Tree
Ministers Reflect on the Subject of Wealth

Edited by
J. Robert Moon

THE INTERMUNDIA PRESS, LLC
Warrenton, Virginia
A DELAWARE COMPANY

© 2015 by J. Robert Moon.

All rights reserved. Published 2015.
Printed in the United States of America.

ISBN 978-1-887730-43-3

No part of this book may be reproduced or transmitted in any form or by any means, electronic or mechanical, including photocopying, recording, or by information storage and retrieval systems, without permission in writing from the publisher.

The views, ideas, and opinions of each article are the sole expression of its author and are not necessarily those of the editor and publisher and its imprints.

To order additional copies of this book, please contact

THE INTERMUNDIA PRESS
www.intermundiapress.com

To my friend whom I consider a neighbor;
a fellow pilgrim;
a colleague in ministry;
a bit my senior, but wiser and more widely experienced;
one who has been willing to share and receive
personal stories of life, ministry, grief, and joy,
with laughter and tears,
over coffee or Chinese lunches;
and who inspired the idea of collecting these stories:

John Killinger.

CONTENTS

	Preface	ix
1.	. . . And Then There Were the Rest of Us TIMOTHY SHIRLEY	1
2.	A Call . . . to Wrestle . . . Regarding My Money BENJAMIN W. MAAS	9
3.	Pastoring Everybody—Including the Rich JOHN KILLINGER	13
4.	For Sale RUSTY BROCK	25
5.	An Attitude of Personal Pilgrimage on Affluence KEITH SAVAGE	31
6.	Do What Makes You Happy RACHEL LACKEY AND JIM STRICKLAND	37
7.	God's Invitation: From Scarcity to Abundance CATHY ABBOTT	45

CONTENTS

8. I Am Not Alone — 49
   TOM BERLIN

9. Juggling Between Two Naked People: Managing Our Temporary "Wealth" Between Entering the World Naked at Birth and Leaving Naked at Death — 55
   ROBIN T. ADAMS

10. Memories Have Us: Anxiety *and* Hope — 63
    MICHAEL TASSLER

11. Mixed Signals on Wealth and Poverty — 73
    J. ROBERT MOON

12. One Minister's Journey with Wealth — 85
    JOHN PAUL CARTER

13. The Principle of the Four Quarters — 93
    DALLAS STALLINGS

14. To Have or Not to Have: Messages Sent and Received — 101
    OLIVER M. ROOPER

15. Twin Legacies — 121
    DONNA S. MOTE

16. The War on Poverty: A Young Baptist's Perspective — 127
    BILL J. LEONARD

17. What Would I Have to Say About Wealth If I Was Warren Buffett's Pastor? — 135
    LOU SNEAD

Contributors — 145

Acknowledgements — 147

About the Editor — 149

PREFACE

IMAGINE YOURSELF WALKING IN THE crowd that is following Jesus. Perhaps you are a part of the inner circle, the chosen threesome, Simon Peter, John, or James. You have the ear of Jesus and can almost tell what he is thinking, anticipating his next move. Or, you are a member of the support team—Martha, Mary, Joanna, Susanna, or the Magdalene. You gladly share your resources because you appreciate this man who speaks openly, honestly, and respectfully with women and men. Maybe you are part of the circle Jesus has personally recruited, Andrew, Judas, Thomas, Philip, Bartholomew, Thaddeus, Jude, Simon, or Levi. Perhaps you are one of the curious in the crowd that day. Wherever, and whoever you are in the crowd, you are moving together as a loose group on the road passing through Jericho. Regardless of your proximity to Jesus, you are a follower.

You see it, about the same time everyone else sees it: a man, straddling a thick tree branch that is spreading directly over the path Jesus is taking—a wealthy man, no less. You can tell by his clean clothes, the fine linen, the plush fabric trim, the deep rich colors. His jewelry tells you that he is not a part of this crowd. It is unmistakable. You know this man, or at least know of him.

What do you feel, looking up at this grown man, a rich man? He has no courtesy, no manners, no reservations about getting close to Jesus—closer than you have been able to get.

What is that kicking up in your gut? Is it anger? Envy? Embarrassment? For yourself? For Jesus? Before anyone can speak, what would you like to say? What's on your mind? Or would that not be acceptable?

His legs dangle down, revealing the finest leather sandals available this side of Jerusalem. He looks well groomed, nicer than the crowd around you; probably smells nicer than you. You are hot and sweaty, feet dusty and sore, for you have been following Jesus as a part of this crowd for several hours now, and this guy has been sitting in the shade of a sycamore tree just waiting. He does not stress about being absent from work, for he makes his own work, carves his own hours, keeps his own books.

He is rich. Are you comfortable with this rich guy? Looking into the center of the crowd, you detect that a conversation has started between Jesus and this rich man. You cannot hear their words because the crowd is murmuring disrespectfully. What do you imagine Jesus saying to this man? What should he be saying?

Words drift back in incredulous echoes: "He just invited himself to Zach's house for dinner." The tone of the crowd is not cordial, but dismayed. Really? Jesus . . . at Zach's house . . . for dinner?

The second wave of murmurs confirms the first, but with no added details. This sudden development seems more than a bit confusing. Jesus has been closely associated with the poor, the oppressed. Is he breaking his own commitment to meet the needs of the disenfranchised? You can't answer your own question, because you can't hear, and you weren't invited to the dinner.

You watch the crowd dissipate as Zach drops down from the branch. The two of them, Jesus and Zach, go off together toward the nicer side of town.

What are your feelings at this point?

What is the origin of those feelings?

Did these feelings come from your childhood, from coaching by your parents about how to view rich people? Are the wealthy to be admired, mimicked, excluded, or ridiculed? Was wealth a taboo subject in your family circle, or was wealth the pursuit of every generation? How was wealth measured?

Do your feelings toward the rich, the wealthy—positive or negative—come from your childhood or your adult experiences? Have the well-to-do in your experience been generous or stingy, stewards or spendthrifts, kind or viscous, freeing or oppressive? What events, persons, or experiences shaped your frame of reference in your response to wealth and those who are affluent? Does the presence of wealth impact how you preach, teach, raise support for the church, and deliver pastoral care? If you were trained as a minister to take the side of the poor, you might be uncomfortable with the subject of wealth. Perhaps you entered the ministry to get away from wealth. Was your calling more like St. Francis of Assisi, abandoning his father's business life in order to care for the poor? Do you wear a Timex or a Rolex as a matter of choice, or as a matter of affordability?

This book is intended to help you understand, as one essayist comments, that you are not alone in your struggle with the subject of wealth. In these pages you will find kindred spirits as well as colleagues that could stretch your views and approaches to wealth.

This book is about feelings about wealth, about money, about resources—a collection of essays, by ministers, for ministers, on the subject of wealth. Some of the reflections focus on childhood formations toward wealth. Others focus on their successes or failures in pastoral care in the context of wealth. These reflections are not intended to make a point. In some instances they are confessional; in others, testimonial. Some reveal that the search for answers continues. They represent a broad range of perspectives that includes some of the major protestant denominations. Contributors include the new minister, the seasoned pastor, or the retiree looking back on a career. In some cases, the author has elected the privilege and protection of a pen name and fictitious names to protect confidentiality. One thing these essays are not. They are not stewardship sermons. In fact, they are not sermons at all. But having more insight about your colleagues, these essays just might become good news.

Robert Moon
Editor

. . . AND THEN THERE WERE THE REST OF US

TIMOTHY SHIRLEY

I LEARNED AT A very early age that some people had a lot of money and were considered wealthy; and then there were the rest of us. I am the nephew of Raymond Parks, one of the founders of NASCAR, a man who made his early money in the moonshine trade. At an early age he became a moonshine runner, eventually becoming his own boss in the trade. He quickly achieved a great measure of success in what quickly evolved into a very profitable business. Moonshining provided the foundation that would lead to Raymond's numerous other pursuits as an imaginative entrepreneur. Like many of my cousins on my mother's side, I was not exposed to the realities of our family legacy until well into adulthood. I recall myself as a child going to one specific NASCAR race in Charlotte, North Carolina, not knowing any of the heritage or relationship attached to it. I thought it was just an ordinary road trip and that we were simply going to see an automobile race. I knew absolutely nothing of the context explaining the purpose. But with the publication of *Driving with the Devil*,[1] all of our family secrets would quickly become public information and thus all of us needed to know the full story prior to the release of the book.

I grew up in a steel mill neighborhood at the confluence of Interstates 75 and 85 on the northern edge of downtown Atlanta. Home Park, as it was then known—it is now considered a part of Midtown—was sandwiched between the Atlantic Steel Company and the Georgia Institute of Technology (Georgia Tech). In those days, the '60s and '70s, Home Park tended to be a rough neighborhood of lower middle class status, mostly consisting of white, hardworking, conservative-minded family values oriented individuals. It provided the perfect demographic from which my uncle Raymond could hire individuals to supplement the numerous brothers, sisters, nieces and nephews who worked in his employ. I later learned that there was a time when Raymond owned every house on Francis Street, the street where I was raised, so that he could monitor the comings and goings of anyone who chose to travel it. Little did I know in those days that many of my negative experiences, particularly the routine beatings I incurred from neighborhood children, were the direct result of being Raymond's nephew. More than once, I was subjected to random attacks. On the surface, there seemed to have been no apparent cause for them, no reason in particular, no rationale whatsoever. Though I never really considered it, I guess I thought that this was just a normal part of growing up in the Home Park neighborhood, a community that reflected a particular culture, a rough and tumble ethos driven by the idea that the toughest survive by learning how to fight. On one occasion, an afternoon beating on my backside was so severe that I discovered blood in my urine late that evening. I was rushed to the emergency room where it was discovered that I had suffered some damage to a kidney. Though not serious, it kept me out of school for several days. On another occasion, for no apparent reason, a family of brothers held me down and allowed the youngest of their siblings to beat the living crap out of me. It was assumed, because of our family relationship to Raymond, that my dad and mom were also wealthy, an assumption that caused the neighborhood children to be angry and jealous. The scenario sometimes would occur like this: Raymond would approach an individual and offer him a car if he would simply drive it to an out of town location and allow the contents to be unloaded. No questions asked; no questions answered. The man was then allowed to keep the car as his payment. One of my classmates once approached me at school and told me, with much arrogance and derision, that his father had been offered a car by my uncle Raymond if he would drive it to one of these undisclosed locations. My classmate was very proud of the fact that his father had turned down the offer. My classmates failed to realize that my father and other close family members were paid a fair wage and nothing more. He and they worked for Raymond in one of his various businesses, whether it was one of the liquor stores, the vending machine company, or another of his entrepreneurial enterprises. Throughout my childhood, our family consistently had issues with our next-door neighbors, including numerous verbal altercations, again, the consequence of their assumptions about our material worth because of our relationship with Raymond.

During the entire time my dad, Marion F. Shirley, was in Raymond's employ, he worked six days a week and never got more than one week's vacation a year. My father ran Raymond's numbers racket, called "The Bug," an illegal numbers game—Georgia's first lottery—from 1945–51, and then managed one of his liquor stores from 1951 until his retirement in 2011. While Raymond made his initial money by running moonshine, it was in the numbers game that he built his fortune. All of the family worked hard with no extra perks or benefits because of the family relationship. And in all honesty, none were ever expected. Nepotism was never the modus operandi in our family system. Part of that dynamic, I believe, is rooted in the fact that Raymond's brothers and sisters were always grateful he became successful and was thus able to help support all of them in a variety of ways. Perhaps the biggest factor was that, shortly after Raymond had achieved a certain level of success and wealth, he moved the entire family. The entire clan was relocated from Dawsonville, Georgia, in the foothills of the Blue Ridge Mountains of Appalachia, to Moultrie, Georgia, which is almost at the Florida state line. They were all still relatively young. I have never been certain as to the reasons for this move, but my hunch is that it was a better all-around location and provided a safer environment for the family of an individual that Neil Thompson compares to Al Capone.[2] South Georgia afforded a much more genteel climate, as opposed to the rough and tumble ethos of the north Georgia mountains. Historically, Appalachia is known for its Hatfields-and-McCoys-like environment, characterized by familial hostility and infighting, and even flavored with a murder here and there. This cultural phenomenon was inbred into the very fabric of local life, particularly among the likes of the Parks and Orrs, the Orrs being the other side of the family system. Together, they comprised a clan possessing a high level of hubris, and were not afraid to throw their weight around. Banjos anyone? Though the plot in the epic cult flick *Deliverance* is certainly different, there is much in this film that resonates. Whenever I watch it, I almost blush when realizing how this film in many ways is a narrative describing the Parks and Orrs back in the day. It really is art imitating life! Interesting and ironic that this movie was filmed in north Georgia!!!

    I must say, that the Raymond Parks I knew as a child and well into adulthood certainly did not fit the stereotype that might be associated with the NASCAR circuit. Looking back, it seems that Raymond tried to distance himself from the redneck image that came to be synonymous with NASCAR. Raymond certainly loved his cars and drove a variety of luxury automobiles, and even had a few classics restored. But those were the only hints that he had once been a moonshiner and that he had been a major player in, and even a founder of, NASCAR. Raymond won the first two Daytona 500s as an owner. Of course, in those days everybody took a turn driving the race car!

Raymond was always immaculately dressed, a regular customer to the late Muses men's store in Atlanta. He was fond of Hickey Freeman suits, a few of which I inherited and am very proud to wear, and was never without his famed fedora, which became his hallmark accessory. Raymond was very quiet and reserved, a seemingly shy man who, despite being proud of his accomplishments, certainly did not flaunt them in any way. Raymond chose to stay in the background in all of his pursuits. Not only was he a NASCAR legend, but he served with distinction in World War II and participated in the famous Battle of the Bulge. Raymond always carried himself with grace and an air of distinction, exuding a debonair and elegant style full of grace and dignity. That is not to say that he shied away from his racing success. If anyone inquired, he would proudly show the numerous racing trophies that adorned his office.

Throughout my career, I have encountered numerous people with money. My hunch is that my experiences are a lot like other clergy. I have had relationships with some that you would never know were wealthy and others who seemed, by either omission or commission, to wear their money on their sleeve as a badge of honor. For the most part, however, my experiences have been quite positive and have even resulted in strong relationships and close friendships. The challenge for me has always been to understand who had the resources to help the church become what it desired to be, while not allowing that reality to dictate or dominate the relationship. I have always been very careful not to allow those with money to take the church hostage in what would devolve into a very unhealthy family systems nightmare. By that, I mean that I have tried to ensure that their giving of money, particularly if they were bankrolling a specific cause or building initiative, did not allow them inappropriate influence or leverage.

As I have pondered these personal thoughts about wealth and

money and how it has impacted my life and my pastoral ministry, I have thought about the ways that Jesus related to money and those who had it. Jesus approached the issue of wealth with honesty and integrity, and seemed to employ what ethicist Joseph Fletcher once called "situation ethics."[3] It can be argued that Jesus was not held captive by a one size fits all approach. There does not appear to be a consistent hermeneutic with Jesus when it came to the way that he interacted with those regarded as wealthy by society. Of the rich man, Jesus required that he give away all of his possessions in order that he might follow Jesus as a disciple (Luke 18:18–27). Zacchaeus, a tax collector who had clearly abused his power by fleecing his constituency to excess, offers to return half of the proceeds he had illicitly taken and Jesus lauds his generous gesture (Luke 19:1–10). Jesus frequently condemns those who have money, once stating that it would be as difficult for a rich person to enter heaven as for a camel to go through a needle's eye (Matthew 19:23–4; Luke 18:25). Even though this was most likely a metaphor used to describe a specific place rather than an actual needle, Jesus' point was well made. Jesus did not consider it taboo to engage the wealthy in conversation and was completely comfortable entering their homes and dining with them at table. Table fellowship was not taken lightly in the ancient world. A meal always contained meaning far beyond that of simply eating, and so for Jesus to be in relationship with wealthy individuals does indeed speak volumes about the fact that he did not universally condemn them. Finally, the fact that Jesus had a treasurer among his disciples, Judas, indicates that Jesus understood that any enterprise, institution, or organization needed finances to operate and a process by which those finances would be secured and managed. In the final analysis, Jesus judged wealthy individuals on the basis of their motivations rather than their net worth. And that is certainly a worthy hermeneutic for all of us in ministry as we engage members of our congregations who are well-to-do.

NOTES

1. Neal Thompson, *Driving with the Devil: Southern Moonshine, Detroit Wheels, and the Birth of NASCAR* (New York: Crown Publishers, 2006). Even though the focus of Thompson's book is the founding of NASCAR, much of the content portrays the life of Raymond Parks.

2. Ibid., 47.

3. Joseph Fletcher, *Situation Ethics: The New Morality* (Philadelphia: The Westminster Press, 1966).

A CALL . . . TO WRESTLE . . . REGARDING MY MONEY

BENJAMIN W. MAAS

TALK ABOUT A topic that keeps on gnawing at you.... In the time that has passed since accepting the invitation to write this article, a fair amount of soul searching and self-examination has taken place.

Do I have a healthy relationship with money? Do I make too much? Give away to little? What is my obligation to the Gospel, the poor, my flock, my family and my children who want to grow up much like their friends? I did not and do not anticipate that my grappling will lead to definitive clarity, but I do think these are the questions we are called to ask. I also believe that our wrestling with these questions is part of modeling twenty-first century discipleship in an affluent community amidst a very complicated world.

I really do not know what my colleagues make in their particular positions nor do I really know that much about the compensation of my individual congregants. Some professions are a matter of public record, but for most I would be hard pressed to even provide a ballpark figure. Consider the countless retirees on "fixed" incomes tending beautiful familial estates, and I have even less of an idea of liquid wealth.

I tend to think that I make a good living. That coupled with high vocational satisfaction and I feel quite fortunate. That is not to say that the money does not disappear more quickly than I can account for it. As I pondered my relationship with money, I first rushed toward my continued efforts to increase my charitable giving each year to affirm my current position. Then I started to look over the vast majority of our expenditures. A lot spent on children's education and activities and outfitting those activities, plenty on eating out (and eating in—it is a good thing our pets only eat in), much spent on experiences with friends and loved ones, a big chunk on pretty fixed "living expenses"; and a reasonable amount putting clothing on our back (but I must commend our restraint in that area, especially given my wife's fashion sensibilities).

We live in a church-provided rectory, but there is the mortgage on our cabin in Vermont. That cabin debt sometimes feels excessive but it is our small stake in a family property that has passed down and spread through five generations. Maybe I am rationalizing. Okay, I do struggle with our limited membership to the neighboring country club. Despite there being a clear non-discrimination policy, it is far more affordable than similar clubs, and it is where our children swim and spend much of their summer. I still cringe when I say it and figure this may be the sticking point that leaves Jesus just shaking his head. I do like to think those dues come out of my wife's paycheck. Of course, the charitable donations come straight from my paycheck.

Listening to all this rationalizing, it is pretty clear that I am still unsure of my responsibility and relationship to money. Perhaps it is just obvious that I am not confident Jesus would commend me for all of my fiscal decisions. Honestly, I do feel my life is fairly well in balance, but

I am not sure when Jesus says to the rich man, "Go and sell all your possessions and give the money to the poor" that Jesus is calling for balance. I am also not sure the kingdom of God is neared through a healthy financial balance. The parables always tilt toward a more radically unbalanced response. That being said, the story of Lazarus and the rich man paints with pretty broad strokes. What does it mean to feast sumptuously every day? How far beyond our gates are we called to notice and care?

I do need to examine the morality of the fact that my luxuries are enjoyed, if not at the expense of, or at least while, children are starving and denied life saving vaccinations and medications. Is my generosity sufficient (which certainly suggests rightful possession of all that I have) or am I on a global scale the equivalent of the rich man and Lazarus? I imagine and pray that the answer to both is a resounding No! I think guilt is no way to respond to God's generosity but neither is unfettered or unexamined contentment. Generosity is a flowing and joyful response, but it certainly requires tremendous work and intentionality.

As I ask myself what it is that I strive for financially, I realize it is insincere to suggest that I want to radically change. I do intend on continually engaging the question, striving toward generosity and greater authenticity when I claim, "All things come from thee." I also recognize that even though I want to lead my congregation by example and stand with integrity each commitment season, I am most concerned with what I model within my own household. I pray my children see money as a gift and not a pursuit, an instrument and not a mark of worth. I pray that they marry all the wonderful things money can provide them with the responsibility that comes with it. I will also encourage my children to engage the same questions that Jesus calls all of us to wrestle with regarding money.

PASTORING EVERYBODY—
INCLUDING THE RICH

JOHN KILLINGER

LIKE MANY OF THE ministers writing for this collection, my gamut of pastoral experiences stretches all the way from small rural parishes, where my weekly salary was often handed to me in a paper bag full of coins, to large, metropolitan churches whose annual budgets ran into millions of dollars. At both kinds of churches, there was an inevitable pecking order, with the wealthier farmers in the rural churches and the big investors or highly paid surgeons in the metropolitan churches commanding the most respect from their very different congregations. Maybe it was the rebel in me—I hope it was more!—that always prevented my believing that those at the top of the order were any more worthy of my time or attention than the ones at the bottom.

I guess, in a way, that I was fortunate that I grew up on the tail end of the Great Depression and, even though my family was as poor as the next one, learned not to worry much about having money or what it could buy. I worked hard as a boy and paid my own way through college, and for years after we married, my wife and I lived on a pittance, for we had both grown up frugal and inventive.

I can't remember that I was ever concerned about budgets and projects that would cost my churches more than they could currently afford. Somehow I always believed that God would provide what was needed—which was how it had been in my life—and that I wasn't called to the ministry to spend my time and energy worrying about where it was coming from.

I do have some memories of the wealthiest members in my churches. It would be hard not to recall some of them. And, as anecdotalism is not only the preacher's refuge from dealing with the facts but can actually serve as a pathway to greater understanding, I hope I may be indulged some reminiscences about a few of those financially well-heeled Christians.

Involuntarily, my mind leaps to my relationship with George Stewart, CEO of First Colony Life Insurance Company in Lynchburg, Virginia, and later, when First Colony was sold to Ethyl Corporation, a board member of Ethyl. George was a personable, humorous, roly-poly little man who was brought from New York to save First Colony when it was in deep financial trouble. In only a few years, he revived the company and led it to become, at that time, probably the biggest life insurance company in America.

George was a member of First Presbyterian Church, where I became his pastor, and taught a large men's Bible class. He once proudly showed me his cozily carpeted study, which took up the entire basement of his sprawling house and was surrounded on all sides by enough books to start a new public library. He spent a couple of hours every night in that study, he said, preparing himself to teach his men's class the following Sunday.

PASTORING EVERYBODY—INCLUDING THE RICH

George was the first "foreigner" or non-old-Lynchburger ever elected to the session of our church. Lynchburg was a town of strong family ties and traditions, but George was so important—and so wealthy—that apparently his fellow members deemed it important to recruit him as one of their own.

George never tried to throw his considerable weight around in the congregation, but it was nevertheless always felt, like a great invisible Yeti, especially in any matters requiring a large outlay of money. Nor, to my knowledge, did George ever criticize me for my much-publicized stand against the Moral Majority and other Jerry Falwell organizations centered in Lynchburg, even though he and Jerry were good friends and he often counseled Jerry on financial matters and contributed substantial sums to the Moral Majority and Falwell's coast-to-coast radio-and-TV hookup, *The Old Time Gospel Hour*. (George was, in fact, part of a three-man advisory panel appointed by a federal judge to oversee the Falwell ministries' finances after they were found guilty of selling unsecured and therefore fraudulent bonds to thousands of eager purchasers across the US) So, in spite of his connections with Falwell, George and I were able to be good personal friends, and my wife and I often enjoyed dinners at his table or rides in his boat on a nearby lake.

Whether by a modicum of wisdom in such matters or by mere pastoral instinct, I never attempted to recruit George to kick off budget appeals or otherwise lead the congregation in giving. By being a friend of his and doing my job well—something he truly valued—I could always count on George to do his part voluntarily, which, by virtue of his ability, was often gargantuan. And he didn't do it only for our church, he did it for the entire presbytery. At one point, I recall, he gave the money to secure a piece of property and build a new presbytery office, and did it essentially without fanfare.

I'm not sure if knowing George as well as I did prepared me in some way for my next step in ministry, but it surely did not hurt, as that step led me to the First Congregational Church of Los Angeles, the oldest and most distinguished English-speaking congregation in the City of Angels, which was literally packed with people of wealth like George's.

There had been a time, in the 1930s, when the church was so weighed down by the huge debt it incurred in erecting an expansive, cathedral-style building that it was almost forced into bankruptcy. But the search committee for a new minister wisely called as its new pastor Dr. James W. Fifield, a radio minister from Michigan who even at the height of the Great Depression was earning more than $150,000 a year. Fifield agreed to take the helm of First Congregational, but only if given carte blanche to make all major decisions and appoint all committee personnel himself.

Over the next 25 years, Fifield turned First Congregational into the wealthiest church in a city of wealthy churches, and attracted into its fold many of the leading professionals, investors, and entertainment figures in the whole of metropolitan L.A. He was a tireless recruiter of people and money, and led the church in acquiring investment properties, mainly apartment buildings and cemeteries, all over Los Angeles.

In the long run, I believe, this had a deleterious effect on the life of the church *qua* church, for it removed the congregation from a sense of ownership. And, when Fifield finally retired, he left a power vacuum in the church's leadership that was soon filled by several aggressive and strong-willed attorneys, each of whom became the leader of a small fiefdom within the overall structures of the congregation.

It was in such an atmosphere, on my first day as the new pastor of that church, that I was handed a list of wealthy donors who were not members of our congregation and told that the financial secretary had already made appointments for me to visit them. The first name on the list, I remember, was that of Mrs. R. W. Seaver, who with her husband, since deceased, had donated a large educational wing to the church building and who herself had been more recently in the news for giving Pepperdine University a magnificent new theater building, complete with ample parking facilities and not one but two campus avenues leading to them.

I remember my visit with Mrs. Seaver. She was by that time a rather colorless elderly lady who was obviously accustomed to having ministers, college presidents, and city officials fawning over her in return for her largesse in their various projects. I drank a cup of tea with her, thanked her for seeing me, and left with a resolution that I would never go back for anything other than a pastoral visit or, for that matter, ever call upon any other notable donors in search of their patronage.

Somehow that kind of thing didn't strike me as part of a minister's provenance, and I did not intend to spend my time coddling wealthy elderly citizens in the hope that they would bestow large sums of money on the church to endow their favorite fads and projects.

Now, in retrospect, I am glad I made that decision, for I have never been able to reconcile such pandering with the preaching of the gospel or the service to the multitudes that is supposed to accompany that preaching. What I did decide to do was to reaffirm my conviction that the pastor of a church is called to preach Christ and help promote the kingdom of God on earth, not to toady to the superrich so that the church can afford the most luxurious buildings and most glamorous programs that money will buy.

I have nothing against the rich, particularly if they are even halfway inclined to employ their wealth for the benefit of others. But as I try to understand our mandate to preach the gospel in all the world, I cannot for the life of me have a higher regard for them than I do for those whom Mother Teresa called "the poorest of the poor." I respect the fact that they often have needs of their own, and sometimes very weighty and pressing needs. I wanted to pastor them as well as I could, and help them to find their way to the highest spiritual plain possible for persons in their fortunate situations. But I did not want to add to their problems by merely compounding their sense of entitlement.

If I was wrong, God forgive me. But I have been gone from that church 25 years, and, though the crowds of attenders have fallen away—

drastically, I am afraid—there is still plenty of money in the larders to keep the doors open and the heat and air-conditioning operating, which, in light of the poor attendance, seems a peculiar kind of blasphemy.

I cannot leave my story-telling without mentioning the most intimate friendship I ever had with a very wealthy person, which was with Thomas Hunter Russell, a big-time Hollywood attorney, a gay man with a largely gay clientele at a time when being gay was not uncommon in Hollywood but was still something of a social stigma in the rest of the country. Tom was one of the attorneys who had rushed into the vacuum when James Fifield retired, and had promised the old pastor on his deathbed that he would tirelessly defend the conservative liturgical and theological stances the pastor had established for First Congregational Church.

Tom had four cars in his garage, a Mercedes, a Rolls Royce, a BMW, and an Audi. On court days, he had his houseboy dress up in a chauffeur's uniform and drive him to court in the Rolls. "It impresses the hell out of the judges," he once confided.

Tom was a trustee, a deacon, and at times the moderator of the church, and he had several minions—fellow attorneys, for the most part—who did his bidding on everything. His endorsement of any motion was a guarantee of its being adopted.

Tom liked me. He had been chairman of the Committee of Seven, the search committee, that had first asked me to become their pastor. When I felt led to go to Lynchburg instead of Los Angeles, he said, "We'll hire an older minister, and when he retires, we'll be back." True to his word, on the Sunday that Rev. Dr. Donald Ward announced his resignation in the church's morning service, Tom called me in the afternoon to ask if I would consider coming then. He was not chairman of the current Committee of Seven, but he probably ruled it nonetheless.

I liked Tom too, even though our perspectives were often diametrically opposed. He was articulate, competent, persuasive, and totally dedicated to whatever he was doing. He had great style, and was always effective when he spoke about anything. If I had to choose only one word to describe him, I think it would be the French word *élan*, which *Webster's Third New International Dictionary* defines as "vigorous spirit or enthusiasm."

Our greatest clash occurred when I persuaded a majority of deacons on the diaconate to move our early service, which was sparsely attended, into one of our lovely chapels, where there would be a greater sense of our community as worshipers. Our first Sunday in the chapel, Tom staged a sit-in in the main sanctuary—half a dozen people scattered in the vastness of a space that seated almost 2,000, with a retired chaplain recruited to offer some readings and remarks, and with no music at all, as the organist was in our chapel. This ludicrous attempt at protest continued for a few Sundays. Then Tom showed up in the balcony of the chapel, where he purposely annoyed the organist during the playing of hymns, and, at one point in a quiet prayer, slammed a hymnbook to the floor, shattering the quiet with a loud noise. That time, I quietly suggested to Tom, the attorney, that, should he persist in such disturbing behavior, we might have to get a police injunction barring him from attending church.

In spite of such disruptive behavior, however, Tom continued to befriend me in various ways. He often invited my wife and me to dinner with him and his partner in various Hollywood restaurants, and usually, on such occasions, would drive us himself in his Rolls, always with a fresh rose in the small crystal vase at the side of the passenger compartment.

Several years after I left the L. A. church, my wife gave a 70th-birthday party for me at the Grand Hotel on Mackinac Island, Michigan, where I spent eight happy years as a resort pastor, and invited Tom and his partner Jerry as two of the guests, and Tom as one of the speakers for the occasion. In his brief speech, Tom recalled, with a grin on his face and puckishness in his voice, our quarrels when I was his pastor, and said that, though I did not know it at the time, he and several of his colleagues always referred to me as "gentleman John," because of my quiet, unshakeable manner in any of our disputes.

I mention this friendship with Tom to say again that I believe pastors don't have to surrender their integrity and dignity to the wealthier, more powerful members of their congregations in order to serve their churches as Christ would have them served.

As I contemplate the whole matter of being a pastor to the rich as well as the poor in my congregations, I arrive at four recommendations that I would gladly offer to younger ministers, especially those just entering upon their callings.

First, be the best pastor you can be to everybody, both rich and poor. That way, you will earn the respect of all the people as a fair-minded person and a devoted follower of Christ. This will do far more to insure that the wealthy members of the congregation will trust you and seek you when they need your counsel.

Be there for all your members, especially in times of crisis such as deaths and accidents, family troubles or misunderstandings, and transitional times such as children's going off to college, parents' losing jobs or beginning new ones, midlife crises, and episodic medical problems.

If you are a good and faithful pastor, the whole congregation will know it, and the wealthy members won't hesitate, any more than the poor ones, to seek your help along life's way.

Second, don't allow yourself to be intimidated by the rich or famous in your congregation. As the old country boy says, "They put their pants on the same way you do, one leg at a time." Some of them will be very proud of themselves, especially if they have earned their wealth the hard way, and perhaps they have a right to be so. But you can be proud that you were called by God to be a servant of the gospel, and you need never take second chair to anybody on that score.

I think of Raymond Aubrey, a poor, sixtyish minister I knew when I was in graduate school. He and his wife frequently entertained my wife and me, knowing we didn't have much money to eat out or entertain others. Raymond was a moderately-paid bookkeeper during the week and a poorly-remunerated preacher on the weekends. I'll never forget how proud he was around the people in his little church who were better off than he was.

Once, a member who owned a general store sidled up to him as he was walking through the store and said, somewhat haughtily, "Brother Aubrey, you can have a pair of socks for free if you'd like to."

Raymond reported this to my wife and me in some anger.

"I told him," he said, "that I would pay for my socks just like anybody else, and that if the church only paid me a decent salary I'd buy more of them than I do."

"I want to be able to hold up my head when I preach the gospel of Christ," he added.

To him, it was a point of honor.

Third, remember that the wealthier members of your congregation are often less likely to come to you with their problems because they are accustomed to feeling more self-sufficient than ordinary members. Many of them have worked hard to produce their wealth, and have thereby attained a greater than average sense of how to get along in the world. They can afford to seek professional help for their problems—medical doctors, dentists, tax accountants, personal trainers, weight managers, house and grounds workers, architects, designers, tailors, virtually any kind of assistance for whatever they need. This gives them a sense of greater than ordinary security, and the confidence that they can handle almost anything life throws at them.

These same people, because they are accustomed to managing their lives with such ruthless efficiency, are often harder on themselves about common problems such as depression, loneliness, and spiritual quandaries. Their self-sufficiency thus weighs against their seeking your pastoral service for many of the problems about which other church members readily approach you.

Be mindful of this. Listen to the sub-texts of their conversations. Learn to make discreet inquiries that might lead to their opening up to you.

Fourth, never fail to preach the full gospel to your people, which, though it includes Jesus' fantastic ministry, his gruesome death on the cross, and his mind-boggling resurrection, also includes the story of Zacchaeus and his decision to give half his goods to the poor around him. The wealthy members of every congregation need to be reminded all the time that to whom much is given, of them much is demanded.

The Gospel of Luke is particularly insistent on this.

Maybe you would like to preach a series of sermons on Luke's lessons about what it means to have money and be a follower of Jesus. Look at how insistent he is on the true spirit of stewardship as he provides all those accounts about the Good Samaritan (Luke 10:25–37), the Rich Fool (Luke 12:13–21), the Rich Man and Lazarus (Luke 16:19–31), the Rich Ruler (Luke 18:18–30), Jesus and Zacchaeus (Luke 19:1–10), the Wicked Tenants (Luke 20:9–19), and the Poor Widow's Offering (Luke 21:1–4).

Then notice that much of the gospel not taken up by these specific stories about God and the wealthy contains little asides sprinkled throughout about the danger of wealth and the importance of the faithful handling of whatever we have been given.

If people say, "Preacher, I wish you would stop preaching about money all the time; it makes me nervous and uneasy," then you can say, "I'm sorry, friends, I'm just preaching the gospel as the good doctor Luke handed it down to us."

I said that I had four suggestions. Now that I've set them down, I realize there is a fifth. It has to do with your own sense of stewardship, not as a minister but as a convinced follower of Christ. If you *are* a convinced follower, then you will often be dipping into your own pocket or bank account to help many of the unfortunate people you encounter in the course of your ministry. Being the minister of the congregation does not exempt you from the responsibilities the gospel lays upon all of God's people to care for the poor and needy. And how you handle yourself in this regard will go a long way toward instructing others—including the rich—about what God expects of us with regard to earthly possessions.

Not only that. In the end, it is your responsible handling of what God has entrusted to you that will inform *you* best about how to deal with the wealthier people in your congregation. It isn't your calling to be a Robin Hood in your church who talks the rich into taking care of the poor. It is your calling to be Zacchaeus, to live with a sense of how much better off you are than many folks and to say again and again, year after year, "Lord, half of everything I have I will give to the poor."

When you do *that* you will understand how to lead your church members to handle their own money.

FOR SALE

RUSTY BROCK

I WAS FORTUNATE AS A child that my family only moved once and that that move was only from downtown Atlanta, Georgia to the suburbs of Atlanta. So unlike many families, "For Sale" signs were not part of our lawn decor. In fact, barring a divorce it was rare that anyone in our neighborhood moved which allowed for long-lasting friendships and neighbors that became family.

Today, however, it is rare when families do not make several moves in the span of twenty years. In my current neighborhood of some fifty homes, there always seems to be at least one house for sale.

Unlike my childhood, during the course of my twenty-years in ministry, my family has made four moves. Our first move took place in the fall of 1994 when my wife and I left Louisville, Kentucky, where we both attended seminary, and moved to Atlanta, Georgia to serve as short-term missionaries with the Cooperative Baptist Fellowship.

While in Atlanta, we lived in an apartment, which was a new and fortunately short-lived experience.

After a short stint with CBF and after discerning God's call for me to pursue the pastorate, we moved again in the spring of 1995 from Atlanta to the town of Fitzgerald in South Georgia where I served as pastor of Fellowship Baptist Church.

The house we purchased in Fitzgerald was, without a doubt, our dream home. I will never forget when we first went to see the house. We walked into the foyer of this two-story wood-shingled craftsman-style home built in 1904, and we were mesmerized by the high ceilings, wood floors, and intricately designed ceiling trim. My wife and I both knew within minutes that we would buy this house. Little did we know that owning our dream house as our first home would be the beginning of our "For Sale" nightmare.

Our Fitzgerald home was such a blessing to us and admired by so many others, that we never dreamed selling it would be difficult; but boy, were we naïve.

In July of 1995, I accepted the call to pastor Northwest Baptist Church in Ardmore, Oklahoma and thus we had the difficult emotional task of putting a "For Sale" sign in the yard of our dream house. Unfortunately, this "For Sale" sign remained in the yard for the next two years as Fitzgerald's real-estate market took a downturn. Fortunately during the second year, a couple rented the house and eventually became its owners.

Needless to say, owning a house in Fitzgerald and living in Oklahoma presented numerous challenges, not the least of which was financial. Thankfully the congregation in Ardmore and some very generous individuals both in Fitzgerald and Ardmore assisted us with purchasing our new home in Oklahoma and refinancing our home in Fitzgerald. Were it not for this gracious support, my personal finances would have taken a huge hit, and, as a result, my ministry at Northwest would have suffered.

Hindsight being 20/20, one would think that we wouldn't purchase another older home; but being slow learners, and having an affinity for non cookie-cutter houses, we bought an older house, and it was a decision we would again regret.

After a fruitful and fulfilling ministry at Northwest Baptist Church and after enjoying our older character-filled home on one of the prominent historic streets in Ardmore, I accepted the call to pastor First Baptist Church in Clemson, South Carolina, and we once again placed a "For Sale" sign in our yard.

Surely this house would sell in a reasonable amount of time as we priced it accordingly. But as fate or, perhaps, Satan would have it, the "For Sale" sign went up in November 2007 and would remain until October 2013. No, that's not a typo! Our house in Ardmore remained on the market for six years. And no, my wife and I will never be asked to host a real-estate show.

Little did we know when putting our house on the market in November of 2007 that in February of 2008 the housing market would crash and we would be caught in the perfect storm.

Once again the generosity of my congregation and certain individuals allowed us to weather this real estate disaster without having to sell our current home or apply for food stamps.

In October of 2013 when we *finally* sold our house (i.e., stopped the bleeding), our sigh of relief could be heard from the Southwest to the Southeast.

It would be the understatement of understatements to say that my perspective on "For Sale" signs changed drastically between the summer of 2001 and the fall of 2013. With each passing month and year, we laughed to keep from crying as the places we called home became financial nooses. Now, anytime I see a "For Sale" sign, I have flashbacks, as I suffer from PTSD—Post Traumatic Sale Disorder.

I think it's obvious that I will never become a real estate tycoon, but these experiences have afforded me some profitable insights into personal stewardship and the generosity of congregations.

One might think that during these eight plus years of having two mortgages, we would have wavered in giving to our church even with me being the pastor. It is with grateful hearts, however, that I can say that we did not waiver, and we remained steadfast and faithful in our tithing. Each week we wrote our tithe check, as we trusted that God, who is faithful and who called us to these places of service, would provide for our needs.

Looking back, I am amazed, humbled, and grace-filled by the abundance that we've been provided, given the relative pittance we've given. Make no mistake, my wife and I had numerous conversations that included the question, "Can we give this week?" But thanks in large part to my wife's strong faith and the example she learned from her parents, we always wrote the check, and we never found ourselves wanting for any essential material needs.

Through those years, I found myself echoing Ephesians 3:20–21:

> Now to him who is able to do immeasurably more than all we ask or imagine, according to his power that is at work within us, to him be glory in the church and in Christ Jesus throughout all generations, for ever and ever! Amen.

In addition to the tithing lessons I've learned from our housing experience, I have also learned a great deal about the generosity of giving as reflected in my congregations.

Had it not been for the extravagant generosity of our congregations and of wealthy (relatively speaking) individuals, we would have had "For Sale" signs in the yards of our new houses and probably been faced with bankruptcy.

During my twenty-plus years of ministry, it has been my experience that people with resources are gracious, generous, and grateful. My personal experience, alongside my experience as a pastor, has taught me that my wealthier members, who are asked to give above and beyond again and again, do so gladly, knowing that few people can appreciate their sacrifices and stresses. In fact, far too often "the rich" are tagged with an unjustified stigma of "being the problem" or "being stingy" with their money by those of us who have very little, if any, understanding of the challenges that "the rich" face.

I suspect it's easy for someone with very little money to think that "rich people" should have no worries when, in fact, the pressures they face are elevated to the level of resources.

For example, one rather wealthy friend of mine shared with me that he is asked each year to donate hundreds of thousands of dollars to non-profits, universities, and hospitals, and he is also asked to help raise equivalent money for these types of institutions. He said that if he doesn't give what people expect, then he's seen as stingy and sometimes uncaring; but the reality is that he often doesn't have the expendable cash people think. In addition, he faces daily business pressures at a level that many cannot comprehend if he hopes to maintain the level of income/resources that allows him to be generous.

In talking with this friend and others who have acquired a degree of wealth, they expressed a spirit of gratitude that drives their generosity as well as a sentiment of frustration about how "the wealthy" are perceived. As one person put it, "God has afforded me incredible opportunities that have resulted in abundant blessings for which I am grateful, and I express my gratitude by using my resources to bless others. The frustration or disappointment I experience, however, is knowing that many people think my approach to life is driven by greed rather than gratitude."

In several conversations, a scripture from Luke is quoted as an example of these wealthier congregants' understanding of stewardship: "From everyone who has been given much, much will be demanded; and from the one who has been entrusted with much, much more will be asked" (12:48).

In addition to having grateful and generous spirits, it has also been my experience that most wealthy people give their gifts with a gracious spirit meaning that they don't expect any fanfare and often their gifts are given anonymously which, unfortunately, allows negative perceptions to persist.

There's no question that Jesus cautions us all about how we approach our money. Jesus says clearly that when we allow our money to become our God and we allow it to become more important than our neighbor or the health of our souls, then it will be easier for a camel to pass through the eye of a needle than for us to enter heaven.

Of course Jesus is speaking to "wealthy people" because in his day one was either rich or poor. In our American culture, however, Jesus is speaking to all of us who are rich compared to most of the world. Too often, this teaching from Jesus is pointed out to "wealthy people" so the rest of us can let ourselves off the proverbial hook.

From what I've witnessed in the church, most of us need to give thanks for the wealthy among us instead of viewing them as the ills of society who are ready to "sell out" to the highest bidder. Time and time again during my ministry, the "wealthy among us" have made sure that ministry budgets are funded, building programs succeed, and missions goals are reached because they love the church, they are faithful in stewardship, and they have a heart of gratitude for their blessings.

It is my belief, based largely on personal experience, that if it weren't for the gracious and generous hearts of believers who are blessed with material resources, there would be a whole lot more "For Sale" signs in front of homes and churches.

AN ATTITUDE OF PERSONAL PILGRIMAGE ON AFFLUENCE

KEITH SAVAGE

FINGERPRINTS ARE PERMANENT AND unique. In fact, in criminal cases involving identical twins, fingerprint analysis has been shown to be more reliable than DNA evidence; identical twins share the same DNA structure but form different fingerprint patterns in the womb. Science further informs of another everyday mystery of life on this earth: No two snowflakes or snow crystals form exactly the same pattern during a winter season.

The probability that two snow crystals will be exactly alike in molecular structure and in appearance is very minute. To prove otherwise would not be easy. Every winter there are about one septillion—1,000,000,000,000,000,000,000,000, or a trillion trillion—snow crystals that drop from the sky!

No two water molecules possess the same molecular arrangement or react alike in the same atmospheric conditions. Identifying identical snowflakes with the same molecular structure and "history of development is virtually impossible."

The late twentieth century saw the rapid concern for the environment that sparked a movement to discover one's personal impact upon the earth. There is a movement afoot to determine one's carbon footprint, or environmental impact.

A carbon footprint is a measure of the impact our activities have on the environment and, in particular, climate change. It relates to the amount of greenhouse gases produced in our daily lives through burning fossil fuels for electricity, heating, transportation, *et cetera*. The carbon footprint is a measurement of all the greenhouse gases that we individually produce.

If science can put forward examples of the uniqueness of human creation, it makes sense that the Lord God would also form humanity with the ultimate example of uniqueness. Science affirms the reality of God and God's creative powers. Howard Thurman posits, "The working paper of the individual is made up of a creative synthesis of what the man is in all his parts and how he reacts to the living process." Therefore, the makeup of my march through life and my reaction toward affluence is as unique as a snow crystal.

The circumstances of my birth into this world helped to develop my "wealth carbon footprint" that (whether known or unknown) affects my thoughts concerning community and spiritual growth. God did not begin my understanding of wealth at the time of personal attainment; God began it at my birth. It came with no control or options for me. There are permanent legacies imbedded within my life journey. It is through such experiences that the exploits of racial, economic, and educational injustices received full exposure to the light of truth for me. The struggles of my parents to successfully raise a family of eight persons in a four-room home were not easy. When you factor in the issues of segregation and racism during those early years, it was a great challenge. It wasn't for a lack of parental preparation, but for embedded institutional barriers in the cultural norms of the day that intentionally precluded my parents from gaining wealth.

My years growing up in a segregated low-income community rich with history and a legacy of social justice were both formative and informative. They left a footprint that informs my view of wealth. My meager-means community educated and developed its own business owners, professionals, entertainers, and athletes. There was always, however, an unspoken awareness of economic limitations. The years living in Turner Station were years of social protests, academic achievement, and community values. This was a mostly rental community of thousands of black residents. It produced great contributors to the fields of medicine, business, politics, science, community, sports, and entertainment. And yet, it was a place of limited resources and finances.

My family and community experienced the pleasures and pains of integration and desegregation. Relationships between blacks and whites during the early years of my life would speak loudly to the failures as well as the possibilities of successful integration. In my childhood I was exposed to the economic inequities between the two communities. Being raised in a segregated society dependent upon cultural and financial limitations left a recollection of unfairness on the adolescent heart and mind.

In my early years, my brothers and I learned to "make do" and found the hidden places of provision—crabbing, fishing, and gardening. It is here where I received the basics—food, clothing, shelter, and security—as well as a sense of and lesson in family values and community. The willingness to share with the neighbor who had little to none became an expected norm in my community. I witnessed countless times how neighbors would make their little stretch a little further in order to take some to a neighbor whose husband lost a job or wife was unable to find work. It allowed the little money to go toward paying rent, so that basic security was accomplished. Although I can never recall being faced with an eviction notice, I knew plenty of friends whose lives revolved around this uncertainty far too often. It is here where I learned that family and community are powerful blessings as well as opportunities to challenge the status quo.

Born in the 1960s, I came into a generation that experienced the vocal opposition, socio-political injustice, and hard-fought victories of challenges to the institution of segregation and poverty. It was the civil rights era—a time of major courtroom, congressional, and public opinion battles. It was a time for taking risks to demand justice and equality for the black community in education, employment, and politics. Almost daily, I experienced accounts of denial rendered upon those within their communities as they ventured into centers of commerce.

Growing up in a two-parent household with five brothers came with many lessons in hard work and survival. My parents and older brothers taught me lessons of hard work, conviction of decency, and continual learning. I learned that life in a segregated community brings with it the "troubled" waters of inequality. I heard neighbors talk of unfair hiring practices and denials of job promotions due to discrimination.

My early years were filled with great childlike joy. We did not let the lack of formal toys prevent us from playing and dreaming with childlike abandon. Our community sat on a peninsula not far from Bethlehem Steel Corporation. It was a usual weekend to find myself and many of the neighborhood children using sand to create the outlines of a baseball diamond on the lot of a junkyard. The dirt was black and the sand had to be hauled in from the shore by hand. If, by chance, someone hit the ball hard and far enough to fly into the collection of junk cars piled high, the game was over because it was the only baseball. Another game could not be started until the ball was either found or replaced. Sometimes, it would be a full week before another baseball was found. We supplemented our dietary intake by crabbing and fishing weekly. It was a skill of patience and community gathering.

I recall one moment of great teamwork on the poor "gray hills" near the shore of our community. Oftentimes, excess and broken cinderblocks were piled and dumped on the hills as a way of discarding unusable blocks. We could not afford tents for camping but yearned to experience the joys of camping within our limited resources. We scavenged the huge lot for salvageable cinderblocks dumped on the lot and walked the shores to pick up driftwood. It took us two days to find enough of both to build two simple structures. We dug holes in the ground and placed charcoal inside to create a campfire. We stayed the night in the structures and attempted to make pancakes over the open pit in the morning. Although the breakfast was a fiasco, it was a proud moment. Yet, there was always that commentary in the back of my head, wondering why we couldn't afford to buy simple things like a pup tent or a baseball or even a baseball glove. Hand-me-downs were mostly what I knew for the first years of my life's journey.

It was not until my family moved out of Turner's Station and across the county that I realized the gross inequities of wealth in my life. My parents were able to save for the down payment on a previously owned home. To me it was gigantic in size. It was composed of not four rooms, but ten rooms and two levels. I would learn to share a bedroom with one brother instead of five. I would experience a backyard for the first time as my own. There was even a utility room and small workshop in the home. For the first time in my life, I could find a space to just be alone without interruptions. My goal in life was to become a lawyer, who would become a politician, who would fight for the rights of all its citizens, as well as make a comfortable living.

It was not until college that I truly began to experience the clash of wealth. I began to talk with many students who came from very wealthy backgrounds. Just as I had an assumption of poverty, they had an assumption of wealth. They believed their lifestyle was an expectation. They cared little for how they spent their parents' monies—sometimes with intentional abandonment in order to rebel. Wealth had become a tool with which to manipulate or punish.

My college experience perplexed me. I realized my childhood poverty was not simply an extension of my parents' choices, but an extension of a systematic approach to common good. What is good for some is not intended to be good for all. Everyone in our new neighborhood was not happy with our arrival. Although there were a handful of blacks already living in the neighborhood, our arrival did not sit well with some neighbors. Many of the white neighbors quickly put their houses up for sale and moved away. I began to experience the disparity between those with modest means and those with meager means in a larger community context.

My family, along with countless others, struggled daily in the quest for sufficient food, healthcare, and transportation. My parents were not lazy by any stretch of the imagination. The obstacles of racial barriers placed before them, however, made their efforts to move us out of poverty a harder task than necessary. The additional burden of racial inequalities made moving out of poverty longer and more difficult, but not impossible.

I neither advocate poverty as a virtue, nor do I reject prosperity as a possibility. If the acquisition and possession of such resources and services costs the economic freedom and welfare of others, however, I cannot but insist on identifying such as systematic oppression. If it fosters consumption at a level of luxury that is enjoyed without concern for the needs of one's neighbors, it is wrong. If it was gained by violation of moral law and deliberate inequalities and then justified by deflecting on the inefficiencies of others, it is wrong.

DO WHAT MAKES YOU HAPPY

RACHEL LACKEY AND JIM STRICKLAND

PRELUDE

IN 2001 WE, Rachel and Jim, were living in Brunswick, Georgia. We were single, working for the same organization, and wondering about the future. Although we grew up in different states, we shared very similar backgrounds—fathers who were civil service workers for the US Air Force and mothers who, despite working outside the home, had similar values about family and home. The houses we lived in were remarkably alike—small brick ranch style. We grew up products of our society's blue-collar middle class. Our parents always made adequate incomes to support our families' needs with a few extras. We were far from rich. Our wealth consisted of strong family values and lots of love.

After high school we, coming from different places and times, took very similar paths. Rachel went to Furman University and Jim went to

Samford University—both Baptist schools. We each felt called to be ministers and pursued theological educations at a Baptist Seminary in Louisville, Kentucky. We each became ministers in churches, even the same church, but at different times. Both decided to strengthen our theological education with a year of clinical pastoral education in hospitals in Atlanta, Georgia.

With these similarities in background—family values, education, and professional calling—it seemed we were destined to fall in love. We did and were married in 2002 while working for a nonprofit in Brunswick. The word *nonprofit* is important in our story because it clearly characterizes our careers. In other words, we, like our parents, have never made a great deal of money. Our wealth has not been monetary but rather in the satisfaction that we have gotten from our work and relationships.

RACHEL

When I was in my early thirties, I made the decision to enter a clinical pastoral education residency program in the Metro Atlanta area. While I was excited about the opportunity to be a part of this program, the move involved some significant financial risk. I would have to leave my full time parish minister role, and salary, for a modest stipend.

Soon after I learned that I had been accepted into the CPE residency program, I visited with my parents. Both of them were children of the depression. My father quit school after completing only the eighth grade because his father had died, and my father needed to go to work to help support the family. Responsibility, particularly in the realm of money, was something that was impressed upon me from an early age. "Always pay cash; turn off the lights when you leave the room; save as much as you can, don't waste your hard earned money." These were the lessons I learned from an early age.

So it was with a bit of trepidation that I told my parents about my plans to begin the CPE residency. I focused on the wonderful opportunity this would be for me while soft-pedaling the financial aspects of the move. When I had finished my "presentation," my father asked me two very direct questions: "Are you going to be working more or less?" My answer was, "More." Then he asked, "Are you going to be making more money or less?" I answered, "Less," and braced myself for the lecture about financial responsibility. To my surprise, he simply said, "Do whatever makes you happy. That's what I've always done." You could have knocked me over with the proverbial feather!

That year of living dangerously financially turned out to be one of the best years of my life!

I have to say that my father's philosophy has more often than not been my own. At the risk of sounding overly altruistic, I can honestly say that I have never taken a job based on the salary. The primary consideration has always been, "Is this something I feel called to, will enjoy, will find meaningful." The salary has been a secondary concern.

I have viewed money as a resource, but I don't want to be controlled by it—either by the fear of not having enough or the fear of losing what I have.

JIM

In the early 1940s my dad dropped out of high school and entered the Navy. Eventually, he got his high school diploma while in, as they say, "the service." Mom graduated from high school with honors and had a scholarship to a small college but could not accept it. She had to stay home and take care of her family because she was the oldest girl and her mother was ill. Possibly because of their experiences, my parents put a high emphasis on getting a good education. My three younger brothers and I got the message. We were bound for colleges somewhere.

The problem for me as the oldest child was that our family had no money for college tuition and board. To make matters harder I wanted to attend Samford University, then Howard College, in Birmingham, Alabama, an expensive private school. The guidance counselor at our high school put me in touch with a foundation that made private student loans. The guidance counselor said, "Let's see if we can get you enough money to attend Howard for the first year and trust you will find a way to stay in school there." In other words, "Take a leap of faith." I got the money and I took the leap.

In the spring of my freshman year of college the pastor of the college church that I was attending asked me to meet with him in his office. He offered me a job as the youth minister in the church for the summer. I was thrilled, but there was a problem. The job would not pay enough that summer for me to return to school a second year. My dad had arranged a job for me for the summer in a factory back home. I could live at home, save my earnings for the summer, and go back to school for a second year. My pastor countered saying, "If you do well this summer, we will keep you as the youth minister during the school year and help you with tuition." His words, "If you do well" were the challenge—another leap of faith. I took the church job and apparently did well. I worked my way through college as a youth minister and then headed off to seminary.

Hey! What is this? Groundhog Day? The story gets repeated over and over? Yep! Here we go again, another leap of faith. Off to seminary and no money to pay for it. I got a job before school began and later a student-pastorate in Indiana. Those sweet people helped me get through seminary. Once again, I made it by the generosity of people around me—God's grace.

After three years of clinical pastoral education as a hospital chaplain in Atlanta, which paid a stipend, I was off to become pastor of four different churches in Georgia over the next twenty-six years.

RACHEL AND JIM

After retiring from church ministry Rachel and I began our lives together. Although we were working for a non-profit ministry to children in South Georgia, we were nurturing a dream. We wanted to start a ministry to ministers adjacent to some property that I (Jim) had been given in the mountains of western North Carolina. The issue before us was simple and familiar—where does the money come from? There were times when we were visiting our little unfinished cabin in North Carolina, which we were building ourselves, I would walk up the old logging road by the property and say to myself and the woods around me, "I have no idea how we are going to do this." Having no money had never stopped us before, so we pushed ahead.

JIM

While we were still living in Brunswick we managed to get The Sabbath House incorporated. We traveled back and forth to North Carolina working on our house and doing a few retreats in an adjacent log home belonging to members of a previous church we had served. Nothing encouraging was happening, however, and I was complaining about this to my artist brother, Larry, who lived in our home place in Alabama. He said to me, "It's not going to happen until you go live it." Ouch!

I told Rachel what Larry had said and she replied, "Well, do you want to go live it?" I froze and then began to crawfish for a few weeks. It would mean quitting our jobs in Brunswick and moving to the mountains with no jobs, little money, and a half-finished log cabin to live in. Another one of those awful leaps of faith. We nicknamed ourselves Butch Cassidy and the Sundance Kid and jumped. We had no idea how foolish a move this was, financially at least. Jobs in the small town where we moved were hard to come by. And The Sabbath House couldn't pay us anything at the time.

Shortly after incorporating The Sabbath House, I made a trip to my hometown in L.A.—that's Lower Alabama. While there I reconnected with an old high school friend who invited me over for dinner to meet her husband, Gil. Gil was a chief master sergeant in the Air Force Reserves. He and I began to talk, and I told him about The Sabbath House ministry we were trying to start in western North Carolina.

He was very interested.

I then asked him what he did in the Air Force, and he told me that he was in charge of the IRT program. He went on to explain that IRT stands for Innovative Readiness Training. It is a training program in all areas of building construction for Air Force men and women in the Reserves. He said, "We do this work for non-profits while training our men and women." I made no response, and he said, "I am going to tell you one more time what I do for the Air Force." He had my full attention this time. He explained again. I said, "Are you telling me that we might get the Air Force to help us build The Sabbath House lodge?!" He said, "I'm telling you that you can apply; and if you're accepted into the program, I will be in charge of helping you."

We applied and were accepted into the program. We had units from the Air Force Reserves come for training in site-preparation and construction for four summers in succession. They stayed in rental cabins around our little town of Bryson City. Rumors in town were that the Air Force was building a missile base up on one of the nearby mountains. The Sabbath House, not a missile base, was under construction. Six years later we opened the lodge. The opening date was August 2008, and immediately the national economy went into a depression. That was not good news for a new non-profit with a bank note. Nevertheless, we had a beautiful new lodge and great hope for our future doing what we love to do.

RACHEL

I could hear my father's words, "Do what makes you happy!"

I have to confess that there are times when I have wondered at the wisdom of my dad's philosophy of *Do what makes you happy* and at my decision to let that guide my career decisions—especially when I watch the financial planning commercials often on TV during Sunday afternoon golf tournaments. My favorite is the one in which people are carrying around their numbers—the amount they need to retire on comfortably. I watch that and think, *Wow! I'm in BIG trouble!*

Wealth is not a word I feel any connection to. To me "wealth" implies an excess of financial resources—millionaires, yacht owners, *et cetera*. Having worked in the non-profit world all of my professional career, I have never made a large salary. I was amused recently when visiting our local high school. In an effort to encourage students to graduate from high school and attend college, the guidance counselor had put up a graph showing the average salaries for people with varying levels of education from high school drop outs to those with graduate degrees. As one would imagine, the salaries increased significantly based on education. I have a master's degree, yet my salary has never reached the amount of the high school graduate! So, at first glance, it doesn't feel like the word *wealth* applies to me at all.

Yet, I do feel I have other forms of wealth—in experiences, in memories, in relationships. And I realize that in comparison to so many other people on this planet, I would be considered financially wealthy. Although I grew up in a middle class family, looking back I see that I was clearly a child of privilege in that I never wanted for anything that I really needed or wanted, in most cases.

This philosophy has had its greatest test and fulfillment in the path Jim and I have chosen for the past 12 years. We have served as co-directors of The Sabbath House, a retreat lodge in the mountains of western North Carolina. As ordained clergy, we were very familiar with the particular stresses of those in caregiving professions. It is now our privilege to serve clergy and many others who come to The Sabbath House for a little Sabbath rest in the midst of stressful lives

JIM

The Sabbath House is located in the mountains of western North Carolina. These mountains were the habitat of the Cherokee Indians and spiritually they still are. One cannot live here and not be aware of their presence, whether on their reservation or not. In that tradition after moving here, I became aware that I have a spirit animal—the red-tailed hawk.

I see them sailing on the air currents moving through these mountains. I often see them in the morning and mid-afternoon circling and looking for their next meal. They have no assurance that a meal will be easily or readily found. But they live with and trust the good earth's bounty. Like the children of Israel in the wilderness, they take only the manna they need for the day.

For the red-tailed hawk every day is a "leap of faith," and in like manner I think it is for us all. No matter how much wealth one has in the bank, every day is still a leap of faith as we search for what we most need—community, compassion, and love. Truly, enough is as good as a feast.

RACHEL

I can hear my father's words, "Do what makes you happy!"

GOD'S INVITATION:
FROM SCARCITY TO ABUNDANCE

CATHY ABBOTT

I CONFESS TO A complicated relationship with wealth. When I was in college, I thought of money as the "root of all evil"—I even asked the older brother of a dear friend how he could possibly go to business school, since all businessmen were motivated *only* by greed! (OK, I was young and idealistic.)

But my problem with money goes deeper . . . much deeper. Early on in my marriage, my husband discovered that I was extremely averse to asking others for money—or anything else. We'd be baking and realize we were out of sugar. "Honey," I'd say, "can you go and borrow a cup of sugar from the neighbors?" He'd protest, saying he'd done it the last time. Even though I really liked our neighbors, asking for a simple cup of sugar filled me with dread. It wasn't until clinical pastoral education that I realized why. During the Depression, my grandfather embezzled money for his family and went to prison because of it. As a result, my family never ever talked about money. Neither did my family ever talk about Grandpa's going to prison—I don't even remember how I know this family secret. As a consequence, asking for sugar, much less money felt well... sleazy.

As a district superintendent, I know that many pastors find talking about money really hard—even if they don't share my particular family history. I am a second career pastor and worked in the government and business world for 27 years before answering my call to ministry. At my first appointment, at a small church of 40–50 in worship, I discovered that there was no habit of financial discipleship. The church was kept alive by the lease income from a gas station (yes, it was an unusual church), and people had come to rely on that money to keep the church doors open. In addition, there were some "angel givers" to whom former pastors had turned in time of need. God blessed me by sending me a lay person who was passionate about teaching people to become good financial stewards of what the Lord had given them. He took up the challenge of creating our first stewardship campaign.

But... I still had to overcome my fears of talking about money—perhaps even for four Sundays in a row! How would I stand up in front of the congregation and "make the ask" when even thinking about it gave me the creeps? Then I read a small volume by Henri Nouwen: *The Spirituality of Fundraising*. Nouwen says that if you are really passionate about something—about a cause, about Jesus, about your faith community—then inviting others to give money to it is a gift to them. Well, I *am* passionate about Jesus; I *am* passionate about the church; so maybe this would work. It wasn't easy, but this simple thought began to move me from a mentality of scarcity to a mentality of abundance.

I remember being on the board of my small college and watching how the top development officer for the college cultivated donors. Dan West was a Presbyterian pastor (which endeared him to my heart). But he always began with building a relationship. Dan took time to learn what a person was interested in, what he or she cared about. One of my religion professors had approached me about raising money to fund a chaplain on campus. We wrote letters, and developed grant applications. Another professor and I got the idea of trying to raise money in memory of my older sister, who had been active in the Christian Association on campus, and had died at a young age. So, we wrote letters to classmates and students of his who might remember Mary. At first, the effort didn't look like it was very fruitful—not much money came in. But then Dan told my father about how we were seeking to honor my sister—and he gave a large sum! It hadn't even occurred to me to ask my own Dad! But my Dad's heart was moved—and Dan gave my father the gift of participating in something that meant a great deal to him. I learned from Dan that money follows passion and a willingness to share that passion with others.

When I lived in Houston, Texas, my church taught me (as a lay person) about tithing and generous giving. I recall being invited to a very nice meal at Pastor Wayne Day's home—along with other lay people. We shared conversation around the table—it felt good to get to know new people. And then a few lay people stood up and spoke about how St. Paul's UMC had transformed their lives, and how they had grown in their financial faithfulness. My husband and I looked at each other, and thought that perhaps *we* should be giving more. We believed that we were being invited into something that was making a difference—and our hearts grew larger. As we got to know Wayne, he told us that this had been a church where a few very wealthy people could always be relied upon to donate at the end of the year to balance the budget. The problem was that those few people also expected a disproportionate say in the affairs of the church. Through Wayne Day's leadership, the church developed a healthier pattern of giving and became more vital.

In my five decades before becoming a pastor, I had experienced people who approached me for donations in the spirit of Henri Nouwen, and that felt good. But I also had experienced people who I felt were simply trying to get to know me because they "wanted money from me." That did not feel so good. As a new pastor, I wanted to be an authentic person who, like Christ, invited people into "new life in Christ." My bishop is fond of saying that the last thing to be consecrated in America is a person's wallet! Dick Wills says that "you can't share what you don't have." I wanted to lead my congregation into experiencing the joy of extravagant generosity. As I prayed and wrestled with scripture about wealth, I came to believe that God was calling me to certain habits around wealth and money in the congregation:

- I must not only tithe, but go beyond tithing—and let my congregation know that I "walked the talk."
- I needed to partner with my laity in inviting the congregation to develop generous habits—because laity testimony is often more credible than a pastor's appeal. When I announced that *every* person in leadership in the church had made a financial commitment, it was powerful. But what melted everyone's heart was hearing from a woman who had lost her job and was on unemployment say that she was giving 10% of her unemployment check to the church because everything that she had came from God!
- Our invitations needed to stress the Christian's "need to give" rather than the "church's need to fund the budget."
- And, most difficult for me, I had to master my family history and find comfortable and authentic ways of "making the ask" face-to-face, one on one.

I wish I could tell you that I have mastered all of my issues with money. But I can't. But I will say that as I read (and re-read) the story of the rich young man (which used to terrify me), I now notice that in Mark's telling of the story, Jesus loved the young man. Even him. So if Jesus could love this young man who so desired eternal life, but was unwilling to give up all that he possessed, then perhaps Jesus loves even me.

I AM NOT ALONE

TOM BERLIN

IN MIDDLE SCHOOL, I wrote a lengthy paper on the robber barons, the early industrialists of America, who all made a fortune in their trades. They oversaw vast sums of capital and wealth. They employed thousands. Rockefeller, Carnegie, Vanderbilt, and the like were men of wealth and power. Pictures showed them in front of mansions, factories, railroads and large tracts of land. I recall that I closed those books, stacked them on the table where I worked, and thought, *I want to be rich!*

By the time I went to college, I no longer wanted to be a captain of industry. Being a lieutenant would be fine. I did not have to be wealthy. Getting a job that would earn enough money to be comfortable became my goal. I had grown up in a solidly middle class household, and I was grateful for the things money could buy. We enjoyed a secure home in a nice neighborhood. My parents had cars that made transportation easy. We took vacations to the beach and other locations that enabled us see the world outside our town. My brothers and I all enjoyed a college education that my parents made possible. It was a good life, and I wanted to find a vocation that would continue it as long as possible.

Then I experienced my call to the ordained ministry. As I entered seminary and began to study the Bible and theology, my relationship with money suddenly became complicated. I became suspect of wealth. Many sins are made possible by wealth and power. Read briefly about the robber barons and you will discover that money not only cannot buy happiness, it often leads to a host of behaviors and actions that can lead one far from the ways of God. And Jesus, he didn't seem to have anything invested in wealth. He was itinerant. No home, no closet, no savings, no portfolio, and no worries. For three years, the more I studied, the less I found to like about money and wealth.

Over the years I have found that I am not alone. Most pastors I know have a conflicted relationship with money. We worry if we make too much of it but we are bothered when the bills come due, and we realize we don't make as much as we would like. We encourage others to give freely and cheerfully to the church and say that we do not measure discipleship with an offering plate. But it bothers us when we discover that most Christians in the United States give less than three percent of their incomes to any charitable cause and many give nothing at all. At the same time, most people seem to have more than enough for restaurants, clothes, alcohol, cigarettes, designer coffee drinks, homes, cars, and cruises. We don't want to be judgmental about wealth or its uses, but we find, in our worst moments, that it is hard to look at the facts without making a judgment. It is only exacerbated when we are attempting to lead the church to do something significant for the poor or the vulnerable.

Tithing transformed my relationship with both God and money. I only started to tithe because my wife made me. When I say that she made me, I mean that she made me. It was one of the terms I agreed to when we were engaged. A non-negotiable. Karen accepted Christ in college and was taught to tithe from the beginning. She knew what life was without Jesus and knew what life was with Jesus. Ten percent of her income seemed a small act of thanksgiving for what she had found. By contrast, I experienced it with the same joy as a man who makes just enough money to move into a new tax bracket. I grew up believing that *tithe* meant "give a little something to the church." My parents taught us to tithe our allowance, but parting with a dime on a dollar each week was nothing that prepared me to part with 10 percent of our small income when Karen and I got married. We were both in graduate school. She worked full-time. I worked part-time. Two years into the process our first daughter arrived. Times were tight. I tithed with a sullen attitude for at least five years, thinking of all the things we could be doing with that money, from saving for retirement to buying a TV set that did not require pliers to change the channel.

Karen would just smile and tell me I might want to find a new way to approach this, given that I was going to be a pastor. Fortunately I listened to my wife. The tithe exposed something to me. I had a degree from a seminary and yet I still had the maturity of a middle school student who wants to be rich. I wanted to hold on to money, believing it would bring me security and a better life. I knew generosity was a mark of discipleship. I wanted to give without losing the money. I wanted to give an offering but not make a sacrifice. By contrast, Karen loved to give away money. Name a person in need or a good cause and she happily offers support. She is an amazing steward of money. She can stretch a dollar further than most and has few needs and virtually no wants in life. She does this, I discovered, so that she can give more away.

Over time, I became more like my wife. Tithing taught me that God can be trusted. Tithing in the early years required us to live on a very thin financial margin that was routinely blown by kids, cars, and circumstance. No matter how careful you are with money, things just happen. When they did, some little blessing would come our way to get us through. I don't believe that if you tithe God will make you rich or even serve as a cosmic insurance policy. I do believe, based on my experience, that God can be trusted in times of real need.

Tithing also helped me fall out of love with money and possessions. The more I came to enjoy the things we did through our tithe and other contributions, the more things sold in stores lost their luster. I admit that I still like things. But I have found the gracious boundaries. I learned that one TV is enough. An old recliner is a comfortable recliner. There is an odd joy to driving a car until it simply won't go any farther, seeing how many miles you rack up through good maintenance and touch up paint. By contrast, educating kids in Africa, helping a hospital where the poor are served, assisting in Haiti, helping a family in our community, and being a partner in the ministry of our church mean the world to us. Doing these things has united me with my spouse and with others who also value the ministries to which we donate.

Getting to know generous people has also helped me look differently at money and wealth. Some generous people do not have a big income. Many of these persons budget and save carefully so that they can share what they have with others. Some are so committed to generosity that they will find a way to make more money so that they can give it away. Or they will use their time and talents to bless others freely. From them I have learned the joy of generosity, and the planning it takes to be able to give.

Generous people who are wealthy also tend to think very carefully about the money they give. They see their donations as investments and often want to know who it helps, how many people will be impacted, and the transformation the project in question hopes to provide. People with wealth can also have a conflicted relationship with money, feeling the weight of responsibility they carry to do good while finding a lifestyle that is balanced. They might struggle with the boundaries of life. They do not want their wealth to negatively impact their children or skew their perspective of life.

Generous people from all income brackets have helped me understand that money is connected to so many decisions that Christians must be thoughtful about its uses. We should think about money more, not less. Thinking is not coveting. It is the consideration of the proper place of wealth in our lives. We have to consider the life Christ is offering to us, and whether our use of money serves or hinders it.

Over time, Christ has transformed the way I experience money and wealth. I no longer pine for them. And I do not kid myself into thinking that they don't matter. The key has been to consider the generosity side of money, which keeps everything else in perspective. As a pastor, I have found that the more conscious I am of the way I think about money and the more joy I find in using money to bless others, the more helpful I become to those I serve.

JUGGLING BETWEEN TWO NAKED PEOPLE: MANAGING OUR TEMPORARY "WEALTH" BETWEEN ENTERING THE WORLD NAKED AT BIRTH AND LEAVING NAKED AT DEATH

ROBIN T. ADAMS

IT WAS A STRONG temptation, and it almost got me. I must have been about eight or nine years old, and I had become aware of the value of money. If you had money in your pocket, which I never had at the time, you could buy any amount of candy and soda you desired. These were special treats, provided rarely by our parents and never in the weekly shopping trip, but appearing occasionally whenever we had visitors who liked to spoil the five children in the family. Mine was a working class family—my father a mailman (postman in Ireland) and my mother a part time "dinner lady" working the lunch hour in a nearby school. I never thought of us as poor or deprived in any way back then and I still don't. We had plenty of food, clothing, and shelter. I remember hearing this grace, which says it well, by Robert Burns,

> Some hae meat and canna eat,
> And some wad eat that want it,
> But we hae meat and we can eat,
> And sae the Lord be thankit.
> — The Selkirk Grace, 1794

    The temptation was that my father, the rural postman, got a lot of tips at Christmas. Sometimes these where in kind, such as bottles of whiskey, baked goods, eggs, chickens, knitted items, turf, and otherwise as cash. The cash usually came in the form of coins, though perhaps looking back the notes were kept somewhere else. Dad "hid" the daily growing stash of shiny coins above the large wardrobe in my parent's bedroom. I expect he just emptied out his pockets on top of the high wardrobe at the end of each long day of Christmas delivery. I don't remember how I discovered the hoard of cash, perhaps chasing after a paper dart, who knows? But one day near Christmas, I found it. To a nine-year-old, it was like Aladdin finding a hidden treasure. I didn't do anything for a few days except check daily on the growth of the pile and dream. Then the temptation took voice. A pile is just a pile—I or some one else reasoned inside my head. Surely, it was not counted by anyone. A few handfuls would not reduce the pile by any noticeable amount, but to me it would be a fortune.

    So one afternoon when the house was quiet I ventured up to the big wardrobe and grabbed a couple of big handfuls of the silver coins, stuffed them in my pockets and ran for it. The running part was not well thought out. Why I was running I don't really know. I ran out the backyard and over the fence into the big field and across the rise in its center to a safe spot out of sight from nosey neighbors. So panting from running or perhaps the adrenalin of the crime, I hunkered down to count the booty. I counted it several times in several ways. Then I dreamed for a while of how I might spend it. Soon this became a bit of a problem when you now remember that I didn't get pocket money. Questions would be asked of the nouveau riche; siblings would notice and tattle for sure. Seems that I had not thought these things through carefully—grabbing and running was the only goal that had driven my actions to that point. Having achieved that victory, now I was confounded by the practicalities of managing my first real wealth! Added to this reality was a new voice, my Christian upbringing. Stealing was clearly wrong, against one of the Ten Commandments—was it number seven or eight? Anyway, very wrong for sure! Jesus would not be pleased. Basic Sunday school lessons were flooding back to me.

With a heavy heart, I decided to do the right thing and return the stolen hoard to its rightful place on top on the big wardrobe. I was not brave enough or perhaps repentant enough to confess to anyone my sin. But the Lord and I had a chat about it that night after the stealthy return had been successfully accomplished.

In my teens and twenties my philosophy about money was perhaps derived from my parents' and relatives' Protestant ethic. You worked for what you needed, and then you could spend it in good conscience. Borrowing was unthinkable, but then so was any kind of saving except the short term saving for an upcoming expense. For example, as teenagers we picked potatoes for the local farmers all summer long to get the cash for our Boys Brigade summer trip. I graduated college without any debt but without any money either. I went directly to seminary and at twenty-five graduated from there without any debt but again without any money either. It was only when I started parish work and a few years later I got married that I thought much about money. Tithing to the local church was a given and 10 percent was easy to work out. But after that we just spent most of what we had. Saving was short-term only, for the annual vacation perhaps or some item of furniture. But no thought of retirement, or wealth management beyond what the government forced upon me. The following verse, rich in wisdom, would not have impacted me back then because stewardship was not reckoned to be part of the gospel in my Christian culture but only an optional secondary issue.

> Command those who are rich in this present world not to arrogant nor to put their hope in wealth, which is so uncertain, but to put their hope in God, who richly provides us with everything for our enjoyment. Command them to do good, to be rich in good deeds, and to be generous and willing to share. In this way they will lay up treasurers for themselves as a firm foundation for the coming age, so that they may take hold of life that is truly life (1 Timothy 6:17–19, NIV).

Paul, speaking to a young but highly influential pastor and a leader of the next generation of pastors, reminded Timothy of his Christian duty in regard to teaching the Christian wealthy about managing wealth. It is worth remembering that a few verses earlier he told Timothy about how to instruct the poor. I guess the definition of rich and poor is rather arbitrary and perhaps varies from one culture to another. My definition is that if you have security in the basic necessities of life then you are definitely not poor. If there is a little extra around on a regular basis then you are rich. Most first world Christians are rich beyond the wildest dreams of the common man in Jesus day or the third world citizen today.

This point was brought home to me in my first charge as rector in an inner city parish in Belfast. Most parishioners thought of themselves as poor, and they could identify some privileged neighborhoods on the suburbs as affluent and therefore probably arrogant to boot. In my experience both rich and poor tend to hold false assumptions about the other group. We organized a rich man/poor man dinner to highlight the contrast in living standards across the world. We were hosting a Tanzanian archdeacon at the time, and he was sharing stories of how his people lived. The dinner was designed to be shocking and it was. Ten people to each table, all paying the same cover charge; but nine would get a simple bowl of soup, self-service style. One person selected at random would sit at the head of the table and with silver service provided, be served a five-course meal of delicious food. The others, after the soup was consumed, got to watch. We got plenty of complaints about that evening even though we had carefully explained the rules beforehand and the reason for the acted parable. Eventually, because complaints can be a great teaching moment and the Tanzanian had great stories, the people got it. The world is still divided! By the standards of the third world, even we in deprived and war torn inner city Belfast were rich in every way. We enjoyed indoor plumbing; clean running water, constant electricity, free education, free health care, and social services. We had the necessities, and we had some discretionary income also. We were blessed. We were, as Paul would say, "rich in this present world."

Now as a pastor, I can say that I have often reminded people about the first part of what Paul says, though *command* is a bit strong for our culture, don't you think? But then again why not "command," if it is of vital importance? Lots of parables and the Sermon on the Mount speak about the dangers of trusting in wealth and not in the grace of God. But what about obeying the second part: *Command them to do good, to be rich in good deeds, and to be generous and willing to share*? The first part is about how to think about your wealth, but the second is about what to do with it. Educating the wealthy about wealth management is part of the responsibility of being a pastor. We tend to browbeat the wealthy whenever the parish has a funding problem for repairs or expansions. This is to make the church's immediate needs, instead of the wealthy person's calling, the focal point. Paul's point was that generosity and sharing is to be a way of life for the wealthy. Premeditated generosity should be part of their daily routine and as thoughtfully planned out as any retirement fund or dream vacation. I must confess that I find obeying this directive from Paul very hard to do. Courage is lacking. Partly it is fear of being misunderstood. I don't want to come off as mercenary. Yet wealth is a trap as surely as poverty. The gospel speaks to both.

A great help in these last few years has been Dave Ramsey's Financial Peace University. Apart from his many great lessons about getting out of debt, organizing a budget, communication about values with your spouse, and saving for the long term, his greatest lesson is about wealth management. Wealth is a tool for doing kingdom work. It is a great adventure, Ramsey says. Giving money to a worthy kingdom ministry or directly and discretely to a person you know in real need is the greatest fun you can have with money in this world.

A few years ago, I counseled a wealthy woman who had lent seed money to an ethnic church to help get them started. Now that it was established and doing effective ministry she felt that it was high time she was paid back. It seems that the church always found a use for its spare income and kept putting off the repayment. There were two problems here as I see it. The ethnic church should have paid her back if it had promised to do so, especially now that it was established. That church needed to keep its word. The woman, however, was not rich in good deeds, generous and willing to share. She was looking at ministry as a business proposition. The loan had poisoned her thinking and made her angry and distant from her former friends. I asked if she needed the money. "Of course not," she replied, a bit shocked at the mild suggestion. It was pocket money to her! Then I advised her to convert the loan into a gift. The church would be blessed and more of its resources would go into building the kingdom among its people. They will bless her as a benefactor and God will be pleased with her kindness—also, she gets a tax deduction, but that's not the best motive. She took my advice, converted the loan to a gift, mended relationships and blessed a young church that was doing a great pioneer work for the Lord in its community. Everyone came out ahead.

I want to end with this great quotation from the Lausanne conference. It was a gathering in 1980 of key evangelical leaders from around the globe who strived to maintain the integrity of the evangelical message while living out its implications with an intentionality not usually seen in conservative Christian circles, at least in the West.

We resolve to renounce waste and oppose extravagance in personal living, clothing and housing, travel and church buildings. We also accept the distinction between necessities and luxuries, creative hobbies and empty status symbols, modesty and vanity, occasional celebrations and normal routine, and between service to God and slavery to fashion. Where to draw the line requires conscientious thought and decisions by us, together with members of our family.

— "Personal Lifestyle," *Evangelical Commitment to Simple Lifestyle* (Lausanne, 1980).

MEMORIES HAVE US: ANXIETY *AND* HOPE

MICHAEL TASSLER

NOT LONG AGO, I heard the distinguished Roman Catholic theologian James Alison say that it's not so much that we have memories, as if memories are things we possess, but rather that memory has us. Nowhere have I thought this truer than in my dad's recollection of his own father, and subsequently, in my own lingering over my father's memory of his father. My grandfather died when my dad was five years old, and my dad's memories of his father were stunningly real and warm. As my dad would tell stories of his dad, I wondered how he could remember so much from such a young age. Was it the pain of losing his father that seared these stories and memories into his heart and soul? Was some of his memory manufactured or improved as time went on? Why was his conscious recollection so warm and loving? One of the results of "memory having me" is my sense of longing for my grandfather. I experience him as warm, as if he were present to me, because of my father's memory. My grandfather was a Lutheran pastor, as I am now, and I have before me on my desk his Greek New Testament, a 1904 edition of Eberhard Nestle's *Novum Testamentum Graece*. In its margins are his pencil-written notes, some in English, some in German. I wish I could sit with him and discuss his insights. Even though I "possess" this book, it's part of what creates my longing, the story in which I am held, which possesses and surpasses me.

Alongside my dad's warm memories, I'm also keenly aware that my grandfather's untimely death set off a wave of anxiety about money that washes over me still. In many ways, I've come to see my grandfather's death as one of the most significant events of *my* life. A Lutheran pastor in the 1910s and '20s, low-paid to begin with, my grandfather was forbidden by the Lutheran fraternal benefit society that secured the financial future of many Lutherans to purchase life insurance. The belief was, in the piety of the Lutheran culture of the day, that life insurance was a form of gambling that was permissible for the laity but showed an unacceptable lack of faith among the clergy. "God will provide," was the assurance to the clergy. When my grandfather became sick with Addison's disease—an illness controllable not long after he died—and died at the age of 40 on the eve of the Great Depression, leaving a widow and three sons, God was given a great opportunity to provide—just not a death benefit sufficient to help make ends meet.

My father described the time after his father's death as traumatic, as well it might be for any family in such straits. A cousin recently mentioned that her father, my dad's brother and also a Lutheran pastor, said my father's family lived as paupers. For a while, the family was allowed to live in the congregation's parsonage. That would last only a short while until the next pastor arrived. My father recalled the kindness of parishioners who purchased his mother's baked goods. One church member, an engineer at a tool and die company, brought chickens and other fixings for Thanksgiving and Christmas dinners, claiming that his company paid for them; my dad suspected he purchased them out of his own pocket. Until a small church pension kicked in and until the family received what my dad called "mother's aid," county welfare that lasted until each child reached age 16, times were very lean.

Five years later, at age 10, my dad began caddying at a local country club, often carrying two bags over two rounds a day. He would throw the 75 cents he made into the family pot. When my dad told stories of these years, there was swashbuckling adventure. "We would clean our teeth by chewing on the chunks of tar that would fall from street pavers!" "We played king of the hill on heaps of coal!" Indeed, it seemed that necessity birthed much invention; the games and escapades my dad and his brothers and their friends created seem like a wonderland compared to the world of kids today who while their time away on computer gaming screens. Despite the adventure, when my dad told these stories, the pauperism leaked back in and a sense of darkness overshadowed the light.

My father received a college education by winning a Westinghouse Scholarship. He attended the prestigious Carnegie Tech University in Pittsburg and during those years his scholarship demanded that he work full-time. Working as an overnight security guard, my father told of planting an alarm clock across the room in the bottom of a drawer, forcing him out of bed to turn it off while a student in the dorm room next door banged on the door at the same time. In the middle of college, he went to Europe to serve in the Army Corps of Engineers during World War II. After the war, he finished his bachelor's degree and went on to study for a PhD in chemical engineering.

My father did very well in his career. He consistently won promotions and, when I was a toddler, took a new job in the Chicago area as the director of research and development for a Fortune 500 company. Enjoying career and financial success, my father's anxiety about money nevertheless did not subside. What I remember distinctly about my parents' attitudes towards money was that it was a blessing that could disappear at any moment, and using it for anything such as, say, pleasure, was courting disaster. Often my dad would criticize his work peers and bosses and what he considered their extravagant habits expressed through the clothing they wore, the cars they drove, the houses in which they lived, and the parties they threw and attended. My dad wore old suits, mostly out of style and sometimes threadbare, and cared not one whit about it. I remember my mom proudly announcing, "Your dad could afford *much* more expensive suits than he chooses to wear." He purchased "used cars" that looked like heaps of junk, nothing like today's "certified pre-owned vehicles." One day, as my dad and I were shooting baskets in our driveway, a recently retired neighbor drove by in his brand new Cadillac. My dad would smile warmly and wave as he drove by, but then turn aside to me and say, sarcastically, "Cadillacs rust just like my old Pontiac." Indeed, they did.

This anxiety came garbed in sound financial wisdom. My parents saved their money. They also gave generously, without grumbling in any way, to the church and many charities. They were models of frugality. We were, without doubt, the last family on our street to get a color television. They constantly lectured to me the difference between needs and wants. Color TV is a want. I don't suppose they thought black and white television was a need, but an acceptable luxury right at the limit. My father would write a check for his beat up used cars. As he wrote it, he would sternly declaim: "If you can't pay cash, you can't afford it."

Looking back, I don't fault my parents for their wisdom and frugality. It's just that it usually came packaged in some expression of anxiety—and even anger—rather than springing from a place of freedom and contentment. The older of my two brothers applied to Stanford University—without telling my parents (he figured there would be a price to pay)—and when he was subsequently accepted and revealed all of this to my folks, my dad scoffed at the prospect of his attending Stanford and scolded him harshly for even applying to the university. When I was 14 and advancing in playing trumpet to the extent that the beginner's trumpet I had been given was inhibiting my development, my parents agreed that I needed—not just wanted—a higher quality horn. They purchased me a Bach Stradivarius trumpet, a professional quality instrument, but made the gift conditional upon my agreeing never to endeavor to become a professional trumpet player. Though I didn't know at age 14 what I wanted to be when I grew up, I knew that I loved music, and I was lying through my teeth when I agreed to their condition, solely to have that trumpet.

When it came to financial decisions, it seemed that my two brothers and I could only disappoint our parents. My brother, who failed by virtue of his ambition to attend Stanford, flush with cash from his first post-college job in marketing, purchased a BMW automobile. I remember my father yelling at him over the phone, insisting that he had made the most foolish of choices and had enslaved himself to debt. I realized somewhat later why the trumpet deal was brokered; my other brother had been a drummer in a rock band. The band, in the mid 1970s, had done well enough, earning a recording contract and seemed to have a steady schedule of gigs. Yet, he had dropped out of college to pursue this ambition and my parents were scared to death of the life he had chosen. He had very little money, no health insurance or any insurance of any kind. They were constantly worried that he would get into drugs and worse and ruin his life. My own musical ambitions threatened to repeat all of this and they forbade me from ever attending any of his concerts. Once my mother said that music was "our family's curse."

The anger could be exceptionally petty. For one nine-month period, my father and I didn't talk to each other because I had made a long-distance phone call to him. Dad had always asked me to call him collect, but I had enough money at that time to make the call. He yelled at me for at wasting my money and then I, taking offense, mirrored back his anger and refused to call him, collect or otherwise. We finally relented at my mother's pleading, but never again was there any conversation about that painful episode.

When I think about the anger that my dad summoned up within himself over something as simple as making a long-distance phone call (and to be truthful, long distance phone calls used to be ridiculously expensive), I see the larger story that I was steeped in regarding money: my parents didn't want me to go through what they had gone through in their depression-era childhoods. My parents wanted it "better for you than we had it." So, ironically then, I was given, even in our family's frugality, very much; much for which I didn't have to work: an expensive trumpet delivered with the built-in punishment that it could not be used for that for which it was designed and to which I aspired.

It was hard for a 14-year-old who had not experienced poverty, but was anxiously protected from it, to know the wisdom of earning one's own keep. What kind of deal did my parents strike with me? A deal to assuage their fears about my future? A deal that sealed their fears even as they sought to insure against them? In their effort to keep me from undergoing the pain of their childhoods, my parents perhaps robbed me of the opportunity to learn my own threshold for pain, to gain personal wisdom in the struggle to learn what is a need and what is a want, indeed to know my desires, wants, and needs well enough. Perhaps my brothers and I made foolish financial choices, but couldn't our parents have let us, in love and in trust, fall and fail, without their anger, so that we could learn wisdom?

As I live forward, now solidly in middle age, I wonder how I might do differently. I have said that memory "has me" and that I have been steeped in a story. I believe that we are mostly blind to our anxieties. We are soaked in a system and it can be painfully difficult to differentiate ourselves from that emotional system. I'm no psychologist, but it doesn't seem a stretch to think that anger arises from pain and anxiety from fear. I now imagine my father's early life as having been a shock of pain and fear. As an adult, I am now grateful for his wisdom, his frugality, and the love for his family that, despite his anger and anxiety, motivated him. Grace and forgiveness suggest to me that he and my mother did as well as anyone might have under the circumstances.

Nevertheless, as I try to negotiate my own anxiety with regard to money or the lack of it, I wonder how I might moderate the emotional reactions of fear and anger that arise also within me. This is very much a current affair for our family. The small parish of which I am the pastor is struggling financially. Even though we have great gifts in our community, financial resources sufficient to sustain my salary appear to be waning. Our congregation is the result four years ago of the consolidation of two that were perceived to be dying. The hope was that by joining together in mission, we could continue and grow this ministry. For the last year and a half, the church has been able to pay me only because we have money in savings from the sale of one of our two buildings. A week ago, our treasurer said to me, "Last month was the worst since we consolidated." Alas, it doesn't seem that the consolidation has prevented the dying process from continuing.

The treasurer's were not happy words to hear. As I consider my family's needs and wants, and consider that though my pay is not lucrative, it is needed, I am filled with uncertainty. Yet, upon hearing these words, I discipline myself to take a deep breath and relax. Shall I become angry and lash out from fear? I don't think that will be helpful. Shall our congregation's stewardship ministry focus on asking for more? Not if it is grounded in anxiety and fear about our future, or just as bad, a deadening nostalgia for bygone days. Indeed, our stewardship team has chosen, after much prayer and thoughtful conversation, to stop asking for more, and to lift up instead in a spirit of thanksgiving the tremendous gifts we share with each other and our community in terms of compassion and service and celebration. We made this decision without any sense of pragmatism, of thinking that this is a strategy that will turn the ship around financially. We don't know what will "work." This instead dares us to ask of God: "What is the ministry to which you are calling us in this day?" The answer to that prayer may or may not include my service as their pastor.

In the Gospel of Matthew, Jesus says,

> Therefore do not worry, saying, 'What will we eat?' or 'What will we drink?' or 'What will we wear?' For it is the Gentiles who strive for all these things; and indeed your heavenly Father knows that you need all these things. But strive first for the kingdom of God and his righteousness, and all these things will be given to you as well" (Matthew 6:31–33).

When I consider the striving for things that so marks the human worry Jesus commands against, I think about my parents for whom *not striving* for these things didn't free them from worry either. Strenuous not-striving is no better, it seems, at alleviating anxiety.

When I consider how my father, when it came to money, seemed so anxious, I wonder: can I be different? Can I keep a lighter, looser grip on things than he did? Can I rejoice in the good things I have without becoming sullen and morose when times are lean? While my dad did not strive to have many or luxurious things, the whole game of "having" seemed to be a source of trouble, whether we had much or little. I wonder: could it actually be fun to live by his principle, "If you can't pay cash, you can't afford it?" rather than see it as some cruel rule imposed by a precarious fate of death and pain. Could it be *joyous* to cast off our society's insistence upon accumulation as success, *freeing* to reject its emphasis on consumerism as fulfillment? I wonder: can I let go? Martin Luther is famously quoted as saying: "I have held many things in my hands, and I have lost them all; but whatever I have placed in God's hands, that I still possess."* Can I cultivate that spirit within me?

I've known both people who have cultivated that spirit and those who extinguish it. Nearly my whole adult life I've served as a pastor, except for a brief period when I worked as a financial representative (for the very same Lutheran fraternal benefit society that denied clergy life insurance!). During this time, I've had long experience witnessing how people struggle with worry, with striving for things, with what wealth is, what poverty is. I've learned that having much money is no guarantor of contentment, and I've learned that "being poor" and "not having much money" don't always equate.

I've witnessed presumably wealthy people express great contentment and generosity. One Sunday morning in late January 1995, a man in the congregation I then served handed me a check for $20,000. It was a gift intended for Lutheran Disaster Response. A week before, a huge earthquake had struck Kobe, Japan. He said quietly, "Make sure this gets to the right people." Presumably, this man, in his early 90s, was rich. I had no idea what $20,000 meant to this individual in the scope of his overall wealth, but his gift was generous, spontaneous, freely given and motivated by serving human need. In that same parish, I knew a couple that drove two brand-new Lexus automobiles and lived in a large, luxurious home. They both had excellent jobs in established careers. They were regarded as pillars in the community. I also knew that their annual giving to the church had totaled less than $500.

I've known people of modest means who have shown incredible generosity. One of my seminary professors was talking one day about stewardship to us who were about to graduate and take on parishes. He seemed almost embarrassed by what he had stumbled into saying, but he got started and had to finish the story. He and his wife had decided when they were married forty years before, out of a sense of thanksgiving to God, to become percentage-based givers; their decision was to give one percent of their income away for each year married. They ate their first anniversary dinner on top of milk crates that served as the dining room table. In that first year, they struggled to make good on that decision. They had nearly no income and needed all of it just to get by. But they stuck by their decision. By the time he told this story, he unpretentiously said that well, yes, they were giving away 40 percent of their income this year. They owned their home outright. Their three adult sons all had gotten through college with at least some assistance from them. They both owned nice cars. They were content and relaxed as could be. They took pleasure in life. It was an honor for them to be able to share. It was a joy for them to be alive.

In my own life, I yearn for this joy, this freedom, this contentment. I have come to see that *striving* and *not striving* can be two sides of a *false* coin. I wish to play a different game. I seek to trust more fully the promise of the God who knows we need "all these things."

My father died two years ago on his 91st birthday. In the final years of his life dementia set in, affecting primarily his short-term memory. He could almost effortlessly recall who won game three of the 1939 World Series (his beloved Cincinnati Reds were defeated 7–3 by the hated New York Yankees, who swept the Reds in four games), but he could not tell you what he had for lunch and, most often, he couldn't recall what he had just said a few minutes before. One of his worried mantras was to constantly ask my brother, who was his close-by caregiver, if he had enough money to afford living in the senior facility that was his final home. "I don't want to be a burden to any of you, you know." My brother gently and patiently assured him that he was in sound shape financially. We all took every opportunity to assure my dad that he could never be a burden to us in any way. I'd like to believe that, being held in the memory of the one who assured us we need not worry, of the Father who knows we need "all these things," my dad died in the sort of stunningly real warmth and love in which he remembered his own father, a memory and longing that carries me still.

---

* I have no source for this quotation. Like many things that Luther was purported to have said, one wonders if he actually said it.

MIXED SIGNALS ON WEALTH AND POVERTY

J. ROBERT MOON

*D*AISY SAT BEHIND THE WHEEL, *motor idling, at the entrance of the grey gravel driveway winding toward her home, fiddling nervously with the envelopes that I had retrieved from our rural route mail box perched along the side of the two-lane country highway. One envelope in particular seemed to irritate her, causing her to sigh deeply as she began to rip it open across the top. Unfolding the letter, she began to read it silently, the serious look on her face giving way to hints of grief, her chin jutting out trying to hold a stiff lip, but her moistening eyes giving her away.*

"What's wrong, Mama?" I asked.

She remained quiet and unresponsive while she forcefully refolded the letter and slipped it back into its ripped carrier. She dropped the column shift lever into first gear and started toward the house, then abruptly stopped. She paused, and then replied, "J. Bob, there is something you probably need to know and I think you are old enough to understand. It looks like we may lose this house." Shock waves of surprise coursed through my stomach and my heart outraced my thoughts. "It has now been six weeks since we were able to make a house payment," she continued, "and your father has not been paid in nearly two months. We have exhausted the grace period. This letter is warning us that the bank is about to foreclose on our house. That means the bank will take it away from us. I think you should know this. I hope it doesn't come. We are praying that, God willing, we will be able to keep it. But maybe God doesn't want us to keep it. Maybe he has something better. We'll just have to wait and see."

We both sat a bit stunned while the motor of the canary yellow and white Rambler station wagon hummed patiently. My religious training had taught me to never question the will of God, that his ways were higher than our ways, his understanding beyond our comprehension. But for the life of me I could not image anything better than this house, and nothing worse than losing it. In the fourteen years of my life, it was the first real home I had, a place we could call our own.

My earliest memories of home were small apartments shared with my little brother, my two grown sisters, and my parents, or later the government subsidized duplex that we rented in South Macon. The formative years of my childhood were spent living over a rescue mission that my parents operated. No grass, no yard, only the empty Kroger parking lot two doors down as our makeshift ball field we used on Sundays, or the gravel lot of the machine shop across the alley after they closed for the evening. This new country home provided seven acres to roam the woods, raise a pet burro and hunt squirrels with our pellet gun. With the brilliant white columns across the porch, the genuine old brick veneer, this modern tri-level stood in contrast to the clapboard tenant houses scattered along the dirt roads between our house and our school. My schoolmates looking through the dirty foggy bus windows at this out-of-place mansion could not imagine what I knew was inside. Polished hardwood floors recovered and refinished from a demolished gymnasium. Heart pine boards retrieved from the flooring of a Civil War-era mansion in Macon and restored to a rich luster paneled our den. The dining room was lined with one-inch thick in-laid mahogany panels retrieved from the private Pullman car previously assigned to the vice president of the Central Georgia railroad. Only a few years earlier the Macon Telegraph &

News Sunday edition had featured an article in the Family Living section, complete with pictures describing the house that Love built. How could God give and then take away such a lovely beautiful place to finally call home?

I opened my door and stepped out onto the crush and run surface. I stood staring at this place that had been for me a dream fulfilled, pondering the news my mother had just entrusted to me, her oldest son, her husband's namesake. Returning to my passenger's seat by her side, I closed the door and then announced, "Mother, I don't know about what might happen, or what God's will is at this moment. But if we have to leave, if our house is taken away from us, someday, one day, I'm going to earn enough money to buy it back." Mother released the clutch and the brake and we drove slowly toward the house, a rare tear running down her cheek and across an uncontrolled grin.

As I PONDER THE MATTER OF wealth in my life, I uncover mixed signals. I had an early and broad exposure to poverty. As a kid growing up in a rescue mission full of homeless and destitute people, I saw first-hand the lowest social rung of a Southern town. Nevertheless, my parents made sure that we never experienced severe hunger, so much so that I was more than a bit overweight as a child. However, much of our diet was supported with government surplus butter, cheese, and milk, and day old give-away bread and cake from the Merita bakery. Even after we moved into the new 3,000 square foot country home, we always wore someone's prior clothing, the first pickings of the used clothes donated to the mission. My childhood observations about money were that it could ruin you, but we desperately needed people who had a lot of it to share it so that the mission could do its thing with the poorest of the poor, and we could pay our house payment.

My family legends about "life-before-J. Bob" held forth that my father was a wheeling dealing entrepreneur who made it big several times leading up to WWII and through the 1940s. His successes were always crushed by some external event—out maneuvered in some contract or lack thereof, a wicked citrus canker wiping out the crop and the orchard, near fatal equipment accident, chronic life-threatening respiratory disease. The family interpretation of all the gyrations between fortune and disaster was that God was taking away success, wealth, and health in order to get my father's attention to surrender to a call of ministry. According to legend, he finally got the message when he was diagnosed with a lung condition that offered at best only two more years of living. Then, sixteen years later, after a stab at Bible College here and there, and short lived attempts as a bi-vocational pastor and tent evangelist, he had found his niche in the ministry to the poorest of the poor, the down and out, society's discards. But his push to be a financial success was unrelenting, tinkering repeatedly with start-up business ventures that left our family with less rather than more, an addiction that followed him into retirement and death thirty-nine years after that two-year death sentence of 1948.

My interpretation of my calling was to get as far away from that track as possible. Being the first in our family line to graduate from high school, I pushed on to be the only sibling to finish a college degree, and then fell into an addiction to academics, pushing for more degrees and climbing the pastorate ladder in pursuit of stable churches with nice housing allowances. In my early fifties, after some career changes from pastorate to not-for-profit executive management and celebrating my two sons' graduation from college, I experienced again the hot breath of impending poverty with more than three years of unemployment and underemployment. Prior to this setback, my professional tack and educational track made me the family success story. With a grand education, relatively high income, a secure home, a comfortable and respectable job, a member of Rotary, I could be the source of funds to get the scattered members of our immediate family to gatherings for reunions or funerals. When my good fortune turned south with limited or non-existing income, I would find weeks where I measured mileage and the fuel in my car to make sure I had enough to go for an interview.

I would skip church partly because I did not want to be in the presence of people comfortably employed and partly because I could not face kneeling at the communion altar exposing my holey shoe soles.

In my mid-fifties, I was fortunate to be employed by a not-for-profit agency that served the poorest of the poor, in terms of health and wealth—the residents of Northern Virginia who battled daily with the HIV diagnosis or full-blown AIDS. As the executive director, it was my job to convince members of the community to be generous toward those less fortunate. It was during this period that a board member of the not-for-profit organization asked me to consider joining him in business. He had witnessed my acumen in business management and my fortitude in struggling against the odds. He thought we would make a good team. He suggested that we start a wealth management firm. Really? Oh, by the way, he also was a minister, having served about two decades as an associate pastor. Really? Ministers working among the affluent? And me, the guy who knows the lower end of the social ladder from several different angles, what do I have to offer persons with wealth beyond my imagination or experience? Serious self-examination had to be processed before I could make such a transition.

Looking back, I realized that for the first fifty years of my life I had in some form during my childhood, my ministry or my not-for-profit management, solicited support from the upper echelons of the community. These solicitations sought contributions, grants, or tax supported programs in order to meet the needs of people without basic resources to survive. I knew about wealthy people from one perspective. I had stood before them with my hand out, on behalf of the hordes of needy people I represented, begging on their behalf, for the redistribution of wealth. Sometimes I couched these solicitations in the name of Jesus, and other times I used the tools of fundraising manipulation. Sometimes the cause was a capital campaign, to build a bigger church to serve the common good in the name of Christ. Sometimes the focus was to feed the hungry, care for the poor, to release the captive from several forms of imprisonment. And I was good at it.

I had to acknowledge that in my decades of solicitations in the religious and not-for-profit sectors I had encountered some rebuffs at the very idea of redistributing someone's hard earned wealth to those who seemed not to care enough about their own plight to get their act together and earn a living. But I also had to acknowledge the greater portion of my experience was seeing multiple levels of generosity and a willingness to share. Quite frequently, I observed that the most fortunate realize how whimsical it was that they were on the giving side and not the receiving side. I also realized that the more some persons could be assured of their own survival—that they themselves would not end up in the welfare line, or die in the poor house, that they had enough to cover the basic needs that covered their greatest fears—the more likely they were to be generous with their over-abundance. Admittedly, the generous did not always approach their giving rationally, asking what was needed, but rather determining what they thought was needed and acting as though they knew best. I watched assets given away to organizations that burden the organizations more than it could bless them.

What if? What if someone with deep roots in ministry, someone acquainted with the stresses of human service agencies, or church congregations, could move to the other side of the giving exchange and begin to help people with assets start the journey of generosity. What do you value? What is really important to you? What is your story about wealth and poverty? What needs would you like to meet? What if . . . over time, we together could help articulate your generosity in a manner that blessed the greater good and accomplished your objectives along the way? I thought this would be a calling I could get into, though I realized I still had much to learn.

Very early I learned that at the core of deciding what to keep and what to give away is again the concern for one's own welfare. This concern is not a framework of being stingy, but being reasonable. Within an unbelievably short period of time, many recipients of sudden wealth are frequently facing bankruptcy—destitute and ridiculed for their waste of good fortune that had come their way. Sometimes the financial demise is due to arrogance, sometimes generosity to a fault. I learned that the mere presence of money does not automatically provide wisdom or generosity.

I also learned that not all wealth is the same. There is the proverbial "old money," resources of cash, stocks, property, or businesses, passed down to successive generations, guarded carefully, invested slowly and wisely. The old-money crowd shows its wealth carefully, strategically, with stealth that often defies observation. There is the "new money," earned over a lifetime by scratching out a business or perhaps an internet start-up that is now valued at several million dollars. This single generation wealth is often exhibited through the display of new purchases, new fun assets, and socking much of it away for the rainy days. There is a third category, what I call "green money." Green money in this case is not related to the environment. Green money is wealth that has come about so quickly that the holders of the wealth have no experience of how to manage or use their sudden resources. Green money can come through inheritances, settlements, awards, brilliant inventions such as we witness in the IT boom of the 1990s, or just life's lottery—being at the right place at the right time.

I also learned that not all rich people are alike. Some are very devoted to their families and think of ways their affluence will impact their heirs for the good or the bad. Some folks with wealth are terrified of money, fearing it like a curse, avoiding its management fearing they will make a mistake. Others cannot get enough, hoarding investments and wealth like a packrat on a documentary TV show. Some few rich people want to use their money to be recognized as a very important person, or wield their money as a club, dictating their will in another person's life or in an institution. Some folks who have ridden the ups and downs of financial life have realized they can live on both sides of the financial aisle and will easily gamble their resources with an easy-come, easy-go justification. What they all may have in common: the old, new and green money, the family steward, the accumulator, the gambler, is the connection of their spiritual journey in the context of that wealth.

Looking back, I became very good at recognizing the role of spirituality in the context of poverty—when you are hopeless, destitute, dependent. Looking around now where I spend most of my days as a wealth manager for successful people, I find frequent struggles of spirituality in the context of wealth. Money does not wipe out hopelessness, though it can buy a nice facade. Wealth can buy you a social life but wipe away some friends. It can free you up to go where you want to go when you are ready, but after you have seen it all, been there, done that, what is next?

In my immersion in wealth, not as wealthy person, but in professional service to the wealthy, I revisited the Jesus of Nazareth, the compass that had shaped my first fifty years of attitudes toward wealth and poverty. To my amazement what I discovered was that the individuals who came to Jesus seeking his direct intervention in their lives did not come asking for him to pay their rent, to keep their power on, or to give them a bowl of soup. Jesus did indeed did speak to the imbalance of wealth and poverty in society. Yes, he did speak to the matter of worrying about what you should wear or eat or live. But I have taken a second glance at the probable audience. In my exposure to the most impoverished of our society, and experiencing some severe absence of all resource myself along the way, it occurs to me that the poor are not afraid of poverty. They are living with that reality and seeking ways to survive. A fear of poverty does not weigh in on their daily decisions. But for the wealthy; that could be a different perspective. The wealthy can possess a real fear of poverty. Sometimes they fear returning to a level of a meager life or non-existence that somehow they had escaped. The fear shapes not just their decisions for today, but their attitudes toward generosity. No, in re-examining the gospels, I was shocked to find the omission of people coming directly to Jesus for a hand out.

What I see, in the new light of being a wealth manager, were frequent visits to Jesus by people who had significant wealth. They sought his advice on what to do about a variety of matters related to wealth. "Help me, Jesus, settle this argument between me and my brother about our inheritance." "Jesus, where do you stand on taxes?" "How much should I give to meet the requirement for the tithe, Jesus? Should it be from my gross pay or my take-home pay after taxes, pensions, health care, life insurance, and holiday pay?" "Jesus, are you suggesting dropping everything, walking away from my job, and following you. What will I wear, where will I sleep? What will we eat? You know I'm allergic to some foods and wine goes to my head." Such conversations within the gospel accounts sounds like counseling situations over cocktails shared at a bar, or over a cup of coffee at the Capernaum Starbucks where Jesus offers pastoral care to a hurting soul, not a quick fix of salvation through the quoting of some doctrinal formula.

One of my passions in ministry was pastoral care, be it from the pulpit, the formal counseling session, or the car ride together with someone as we made our way to meeting. What I have come to embrace in my current position is a passion for pastoral care in the most neglected area of our population, those with resources sometimes beyond our capacity to comprehend, but seeking solutions about life's journey, spiritual answers that sometimes are common to every economic stratum, but also peculiar to having wealth at one's disposal.

I also have come to realize how values change over time, particularly when it comes to possessions. Shifts occur in our thinking about what is important to us. Sometimes it shifts toward improvements—moving toward generosity when one realizes her basic needs are met. Sometimes it shifts toward fear. "What will happen to me in the end, will I have enough for me?" "I fear being destitute at the end after having spent a life surrounded by the things that make me happy." "Will my life's partner have enough to live alone or to move forward to make new relationships as meaningful as ours, or to have the option for either?" I just saw this paradigm shift in my own life.

*R*ECENTLY REMARRIED AFTER HAVING BEEN *widowed, I take the opportunity this summer to give my new bride the tour of my early background. I had been gracious and sincerely interested in all the things around Pittsburgh that had shaped her life. It is now my turn to introduce Mariann to fried green tomatoes, fresh peaches, pecan pie, and southern fried chicken as we make our way through Georgia and the heart of the South. I speed along Georgia 57, eager to let her see the showcase residence that gave me so much pleasure in my childhood. We pull off the once-narrow road that is now a divided four-lane highway and onto the grey gravel. The expanded right-of-way has shortened by half the length of the driveway. With the white Honda Accord idling at the entrance, we look through the trees and there it is—the tri-level old brick 3,000-square-foot structure, still in fair shape with its white trim, stately Corinthian columns, surrounded by massive pines but a much smaller lawn. Seeing no evidence of anyone being at home at this mid-afternoon hour, I quietly press the car up the driveway and around to the back of the home. The occupants and owners for the past fifty years have made several changes to the landscape, but the essence is still the same. From the comfort our closed car we examine the front porch and the shrubbery as we follow the driveway, circling around to the back door. There we notice, to our surprise, a realtor's combination lock box on the back door. The house is for sale! My teenaged commitment to my mother fifty years ago on this same spot flashes through my mind. I make some quick calculations. I can afford the down payment with the cash in our bank account. My credit score and income can easily justify the mortgage payment. I look at the realtor's combination lock again but realize that I am no longer interested. My values have shifted over the years. I am still sorting out the signals and my responses to the subject of wealth in my life, my ministry, and my community. And I realize through my personal and professional experiences that they* *are constantly changing. I continue to redefine wealth, success, or security for me, and for those I serve.*

ONE MINISTER'S JOURNEY WITH WEALTH

JOHN PAUL CARTER

RATHER THAN WRITE ABOUT THE impact of wealth or its lack on the lives of people that I have known or counseled, I've chosen to briefly tell the story of my own experiences with wealth over the last 76 years.

Growing up in the 1940s and '50s as an adopted only child in a middle class family where both parents worked full-time, I never thought much about wealth. Most of my friends at school and church were in the same economic category. I worked every summer and when I turned 16 my dad took out a loan at the bank to buy me an old green Studebaker. When it came to money, I was never envious of others' affluence. So when I felt called to the Baptist ministry at 14, I assumed that future wealth was out of the question but that God would take care of all my needs—which he has.

Life changed for me as a college student when I fell in love with the youngest daughter of an independent oilman. Although his wealth was not in the category of some Texas tycoons, it was more than adequate to generously support himself and his three children, two of whom worked for his company in which she was already a "silent partner." Her family, who readily accepted me, was close and spent much of their leisure time together at their nearby lake house. I was in awe of their affluent lifestyle and generosity.

We married ten days after I graduated from Baylor and moved to Fort Worth where I enrolled in seminary and she at TCU. Her money allowed us to concentrate on our education for the next two years without having outside jobs. All the while we were careful not to appear better off than our fellow students. (At one point her father wanted to buy us a color TV, which we refused.) After she finished her degree, she taught at a nearby middle school and I pastored a small church in northeast Texas on the weekends.

Her father died of a sudden heart attack shortly before I finished seminary and his estate provided the money for us to go abroad to continue my theological studies. After returning to the states, our two children were born, and I pastored a church in a small west Texas town. Four years later, I felt the need of further pastoral counseling training and, financed by her inheritance, we moved back to Fort Worth. Later she went back to the university and also opened a small gift shop near the campus. Upon my graduation, I served for seven years as the minister of pastoral care at a large downtown Baptist church in the city.

On the brink of burnout, I resigned and joined an affluent friend who was opening a pastoral care center in the mid-cities. Once again her family's money enabled us to make this transition without economic stress. But three years later, by mutual consent, our twenty-two year marriage ended in an uncontested divorce. Now, self-employed, I returned to the middle class minus my economic safety net.

Looking back on that period of my life, I'm grateful beyond words for the benefits of the wealth we shared. It paid for our education and experiences in the wider world. Whenever we needed money for a car, the down payment on a house, vacations, or the children's education, it was just a phone call away. When tax time rolled around, we sent our records and receipts to the company accountant. Almost always we received a generous refund because of the company's business deductions. Our health insurance was also covered in the company policy.

Because of the extra money and our agreement to minimize the disruption of our children's lives (if that's ever possible), even our divorce was somewhat easier. It left us both able to survive financially—she from her family's wealth and I from my counseling practice.

Who knows all the reasons any marriage fails or what part wealth or the lack of it might have played in our divorce? At times, I felt unneeded and under-valued. And we were certainly less dependent on our partnership. Because of her wealth she was able to maintain the affluent lifestyle to which she was accustomed. I believe that wealth created the illusion that we could have it all. As a result, we probably bit off more than we could chew.

Looking back, even though wealth provided many benefits, not the least of which was opportunity and economic security, it turned out to be a mixed blessing. In no way does this imply that we were the victims of our wealth. And just because we were unable to successfully get through the needle's eye of which Jesus warned, doesn't mean, with God's help, that it can't be done!

For the next eleven years I was single and self-employed as a licensed counselor in private practice, leasing an office in my friend's counseling center. Because of the limitation of fees by insurance companies and the tax burden of being self-employed, it became increasingly difficult to make ends meet. I found myself doing what I loved but slipping deeper into debt each year. Although my child support was reasonable, it also added to the strain. I learned the hard lesson of what it was to survive awaiting "the check in the mail," avoiding paying bills until the last minute, exhausting my savings, selling what little gold I had for pennies on the dollar, and sometimes living on credit cards. My lack of money, added to the pain of divorce, made it the most difficult time of my life.

I also developed a deep appreciation, however, for those who live economically from day to day. And although during that time my church attendance was sporadic, the Psalms became my daily prayer book.

Then my fortunes changed—a friend offered me a job as a case manager in his growing managed mental health company, where I worked until my retirement. At the same time, I reconnected with a lady who was a close friend from my youth, whom I hadn't seen for thirty years. She was a retired schoolteacher and divorced. We were married two years later and moved to Weatherford, west of the Metroplex. Almost twenty happy years have followed.

Today, her teacher retirement and my social security provide us with a modest fixed income. We live from month to month, anxiously awaiting our automatic deposited checks. There is very little margin for major emergencies or some of the frills we once enjoyed. Our freedom to give to the causes that we support is also severely limited. Because of life insurance, I'm worth more dead than alive. And if it weren't for Medicare, who knows whether we'd still have our health or even be here.

All that said, my long journey through life as a child, husband, father, friend, minister, therapist, and human being has taught me many lessons about wealth. It can provide a measure of material security and be used for great good in meeting human need. Jesus, however, was right to warn us that material wealth is extremely dangerous. Its seductive nature makes it easy for it to become the chief purpose of life and create a dependency that leads to greed.

Today, I'm alarmed by the impact of big money on our politics. The rapid accumulation of wealth by corporations and the top one percent of our population, along with low wages and growing poverty is deeply troubling to me. Yet I confess that I am reluctant to lower my lifestyle by paying more for American-made goods and higher taxes. And I surely want our pension funds to grow quickly.

Honestly, even with the wealth that I don't enjoy, when I view the world through a wide-angle lens, I must admit that compared to most of the world's people I am wealthy—and always have been. I am the rich young ruler and the farmer who built bigger barns. Informed by faith, my troubled conscience asks, "How much is enough?"

Now the time has come in our lives to downsize. Many of those treasures that we accumulated and valued in the past have become an almost overwhelming burden. At this stage of life we realize more than ever that our real wealth now is where it actually has been all the time—in our companionship, family, friends, faith, and the gift of life itself!

❖ ❖ ❖ ❖ ❖

Shortly after we married and moved to our present home, the local newspaper asked me to write a faith column for its Friday editions. It's called "Notes from the Journey." When I write about wealth and money, because I don't know who might read it, I usually approach the subject in a way that could be helpful whatever a person's level of wealth. The following piece, written during tax season, is an example of my approach:

How Much Does It Cost?

That time of year has rolled around again—much to my chagrin. The taxman cometh! It's time to rummage through my checkbook and receipts to gather figures so that my accountant can prepare a report of my doings for Uncle Sam. I always dread it, not only because I'm afraid that I'll have to pay additional taxes, but also because it reminds me of how little margin there is between our income and outgo. When I see the final figures, I'm never sure whether I'm a financial failure or a miracle worker!

The other day, as an act of avoidance, I was reading Thoreau's *Walden*. But instead of allowing me to escape into the woods, Henry reminded me of the high cost of food, clothing, shelter, fuel, and the comforts of life. And he didn't even have a car payment! For example, Thoreau estimated that the average house cost eight hundred dollars and that the average wage was one dollar a day. In a time when life expectancy was somewhat less than today, he reckoned that a person would spend more than half his life paying for "his wigwam." But the sojourner from Walden Pond really got my attention when he pointed out, "The cost of a thing is the amount of life which is required to be exchanged for it, immediately or in the long run."

Today most of us labor in exchange for money with which we buy the things that we need and want. But what if we computed the cost of those things—our house, clothes, food, transportation, taxes, and entertainment—in "life cost" rather than dollars and cents? Because we so often think only in monetary terms, our life cost is often obscured. The real price that we pay for things is our time, our energy, our physical labor, and our mental effort. When you add to that the neglect of other important things for which we have neither remaining time nor energy, the cost climbs even higher.

John Ruskin reminds us, "There is no wealth but life." Life—the time we are given here on this earth—is our most precious possession. This one essential gift, that we neither caused nor earned, is simply given to us by a gracious God for our use. And we dare not take this unspeakable gift of life for granted, for none of us knows how much life we have to spend.

Jesus once told the story of a foolish man who spent all his energies building bigger barns to store his crops, thinking that security could be found in such abundance. But unexpectedly his life was taken from him and his wealth was rendered meaningless. "A man's life," Jesus warned, "does not consist in the abundance of his possessions" (Luke 12:13–21).

As I examine my spending habits, the real question is, "How much life does it cost?" Another question follows, "Is what I'm buying with my life, for myself, and those who are in my care, worth the price that I'm paying?"

"Oh, Lord, as I look at my income and expenditures for another year, help me to ask if I've gotten my life's worth as well as my money's worth. Amen."

THE PRINCIPLE OF THE FOUR QUARTERS

DALLAS STALLINGS

WEALTH. WHAT IS IT? How is it measured? When does one know that he has enough? Does wealth simply mean that one has a lot of money?

All good questions, of course, and each of them can only be answered by us individually as we reflect on the very personal value we place on the whole of our assets. My own understanding of the meaning and measure of wealth has evolved over a lifetime. In many ways, even now that I am retired, the concept of wealth, my wealth, is continuing to evolve. The following paragraphs will define my journey toward coming to terms with what I have accumulated, how I have accumulated it, how I have used it and the values that I have assigned to it along the way, all of which have formed my attitude toward wealth. It all begins with my developing understanding of and my evolving appreciation of the value and purpose of money.

I was first made aware that society in general has historically placed a value on money and wealth when I was about five years old. I remember how my father would come home from work on a Friday afternoon with his pay envelope, which represented the value placed on his work for the whole of that week. Pay envelopes in those days contained cash money, not checks, and as a usual thing, each individual from the lowest wage earner to the middle management of the firm was paid in cash.

My father followed a familiar routine with the contents in his envelope. He kept a small box in the nightstand next to his bed with the word "church" penciled on it and he would count out ten percent from the total amount of his pay and put it in the "church" box. He would then give my mother a certain amount that she placed in a Kerr canning jar on a shelf in the kitchen, which was to provide groceries for the next week, the weekly life insurance payment and other necessities that the family might have. My father would then allocate the amount needed for the electric, water and phone bills that would arrive at the end of the month and set that aside. A portion was placed in the family savings. It was a routine that went like clockwork and the impression that I was left with was that money made things happen, made food on the table possible, that some was to be given away like that consigned to the "church" box, and some was to be put aside in savings for things that might be needed some time in the future. There was never any explanation. It just always happened.

When I was about ten years old and my sister was about eight, my parents began to give us a weekly allowance that came out of that pay envelope. Our allowance was always the same: four quarters. But that allowance came with specific instructions. We were to place one quarter in our church envelope, one quarter we were to carry down to the local bank on Saturday morning and deposit it in our savings account and the other two quarters we were free to use as we saw fit. (Can you imagine a bank today that would even bother with a child's quarter?) And we soon learned the hard way that the two quarters for our personal use, like the money in my father's pay envelope, had to last the entire week. There was never any supplement if we spent out before the week was over. The important thing about this pattern was that my parents began to teach us about stewardship by example, not with words. It was a pattern that has influenced my attitude toward money in general and wealth in particular. I call this lesson learned early on in life *The Principle of the Four Quarters*.

My next informing relationship with the value placed on money came about that same time. My first *job* had to do with watermelons. I would work along side my father and the hired help harvesting the watermelons on the farm. I drove the tractor while others loaded the melons in the trailer, and then I counted them as they were loaded for the market on the tractor-trailer. But some of the watermelons had little spots on them that meant that they would spoil before they could reach the market in some distant city, and so I was allowed to carry them home and sell them in our neighborhood. I would go up and down the streets in our community, pulling my wagon, announcing that I had watermelons for sale and usually I got between thirty and fifty cents for each of them. But all of that money was not profit. I was charged ten cents for each watermelon and the money I earned had to meet the test of the Principle of the Four Quarters. That meant that in addition to paying for the melons, I was expected to put aside my tithe for the church and take some of my earnings to the bank for my savings account. From this experience I learned that one has to make an investment before he can earn. That investment might be paying for a product to sell as in the case of the watermelons or providing some form of work that brought with it monetary rewards. In either case, I was responsible for using my assets in a way that made my earnings meet a variety of needs: pay for the produce, use some for personal needs, give some to charity, and save some.

Not long after that experience I was considered old enough to work in the tobacco field pulling the leaves for curing. I never did like this job but it, too, came with important lessons about values and the meaning of wealth. I remember the first time I was paid for my work; the foreman of the farm called out each laborer's name and announced the same amount of earnings for that day's work. When my name was called and the amount announced, my father said something like, "Well, we'll give him a little less today since it is his first day of doing this work." Well, you could have seen the steam boiling. After all, it was a long day of dirty work. It was hot. The tobacco sap burned and I thought I had done a good enough job to be paid like the rest.

That evening at dinner when I finally got enough nerve to complain, my father reminded me that actually I had gotten paid more than all the rest. He reminded me that I had a warm shelter in which to live, food regularly on the table for me to enjoy, clothing that was provided me, and that I lived in a family that loved me, and that a part of living in a family was that I had a responsibility to share in the work load that provided all of that for me. He also reminded me that I should treat my earnings with care, which implied that he expected me to apply the Principle of the Four Quarters to what I had earned that day. It was years later that it occurred to me that Jesus' parable of the workers in the vineyard actually applied to me in that case. Remember how in the parable, Jesus told of the hired help coming to the field at different times of the day and yet when the day was over, the owner of the vineyard paid each laborer the same amount and how those hired early in the day complained only to hear the owner remind them that the pay was his to distribute as he saw fit because the field, the harvest and the money for paying the wages all belonged to him; and that he was free to practice an economy of generosity toward those who had come to work late in the day if that was his desire. In my case, I was being provided more than the rest who worked that day. A new sense of value that grew out of the entirety of my personal assets, food, clothes, shelter, and income, began to mold my attitude toward money and my other obligations that came with living in a family.

I remember my high school years when I was allotted two acres of my own to farm, one acre of peanuts and one acre of corn. This experience gave me a new perspective on the meaning and value of personal wealth. There were ground rules, of course. I was expected to keep an accurate record of the expenses incurred in farming this small acreage. Like other farmers, I had to pay for fertilizer, plowing, and rent for the two acres. My personal labor was not rewarded during the growing season. My challenge was to see the crops through from beginning to harvest. In truth, I liked this arrangement because it meant that I could control, within limits, the outcome of my efforts, a principle that would mold the remainder of my work life. There was something very pleasing about this experience, and, in truth, it gave me a sense of personal wealth to have seen this project through from day one. And my personal attitude toward the value and meaning of my assets was somehow formed more concretely through this experience. I took pride in following the formula of the Principle of the Four Quarters, but now with a broader appreciation of the purpose behind it.

During middle and high school I also worked in a grocery store. At first I bagged groceries, what we would call an entry-level job. My pay came in an envelope just as had my father's all those years before. And without even considering any other options, I found myself, out of habit, dividing my income according to the Principle of the Four Quarters: some for my clothes and spending money, some for my offering at the church and some went into my savings account. As I continued to work in the grocery store and as I advanced to greater responsibility: stocking the shelves, working at the cash register, working in produce, my income grew but my attitude toward my earnings remained the same. I would use some of it for my personal needs, give some to charity, and save a little more. My attitude toward money and wealth was now pretty much established.

Now, lest the reader gets the idea that my life has been all work and no play, let me hasten to report that I enjoyed a normal childhood with lots of middle and high school sports, scouting (reaching the rank of Eagle Scout), piano, and youth group. My time was fully engaged, which was a good thing. The above paragraphs are intended merely to demonstrate how a pattern was set early in my life regarding money and its purpose.)

The struggle for me came when, just out of seminary, I had my first job as a pastor. Married and now with a child, my income did not seem to go as far as it once did. It became harder and harder to save. It bothered me that people whom I knew to be far better off than we were, didn't seem to feel the same level of financial responsibility for the work of the church as I did. And, I'll admit, during those early years in the pastorate, I would get discouraged as I saw peers in our community who had no better education than I making sometimes more than twice what I was earning. And at times the Principle of the Four Quarters didn't seem to work for me because I had lost sight of the attitude that I had developed toward the meaning of work and reward. First, the savings from my income suffered. Next, my gifts to the church and other charities declined. And, truth be told, this new attitude toward money bothered me a great deal. In many ways this became a dark time in my life. It affected everything I was about. Our expenses seemed to outweigh our ability to manage. Something had to change and that change was my attitude toward what I earned and how I was to make the best use of it. This took both practical and spiritual work, neither of which was easy at that time in my life. I have learned since that many, many families have this same struggle. In fact, one of the hardest lessons for any of us to learn is how to live within our means and live happily within our means. We are all tempted in so many ways to think that we would be happier if we had more. But often having more demands even more if we allow our attitudes toward money and its value to us to dominate both our understanding and the use of our wealth. I am convinced more and more that wealth has not so much to do with how much we accumulate but how we manage, how we use, what we have.

Now that we are retired we have a whole new attitude toward what we have and how we are to use it. We are very comfortable, my wife and

I, not because we have more than our neighbor, not because we are rich as society measures wealth, but because we have learned to use our assets without fear of not having enough. We are comfortable because of the people along the way who have had a hand in what we now have: people who taught us to respect money but not be controlled by it, my parents who taught me how to manage what I have, churches who saw to it that retirement income was set aside, a financial adviser who showed us how we could put even more into our retirement account while employed full time rather than simply rely on what the church was setting aside for me, my wife's income, and now retirement, from a career as a public school teacher. And basic to it all, I contend, at least to me, was the early introduction of the Principle of the Four Quarters as a primary attitude toward earning, saving, sharing the primary Principle, which we followed as a family.

In retirement, we have chosen to continue the pattern of the Principle of the Four Quarters even though we now live on a fixed income. The principle gives both a pattern and a purpose to what we have accumulated. We still save for special and unforeseen needs, though we do not save as much as before. We still allocate a certain amount for daily needs and expenses. And we still give some away. Now, we have chosen to support a select group of charities and nonprofits that we feel support the community's needs on a broad base, things that add quality to the greater good of the community. We like the work of Habitat for Humanity and support the building of homes for those who need them. That support translates for us into an investment in people and families who live in poverty yet work hard everyday. And the fact that they also have to invest their time in building their homes makes our gift even more meaningful to us. It is like our wealth, financial gifts and hands on work, combined with their hands on participation in building their homes, creates an affirmation of those families as worthy.

I serve on the board of the local symphony and we support it both financially and with volunteer hours each month. We both like our local museums and make contributions to their work because we believe that the arts are important to creating a better quality of life in the community.

I support a religious retreat in the mountains of North Carolina which I had a part in establishing and which I know offers a time of spiritual retreat for people from all walks of life whose lives are stressful and who are in search for meaning for their lives.

My favorite charity is the Rotary International Foundation and I actively support it because of the kinds of things it promotes: the eradication of polio in the world, clean water for villages around the world where disease is a major problem because of the condition of their local water, healthcare in places where none has been available, and reading/education development both in low income areas in our city and around the world where poverty has limited the availability of a good education.

Life has also been fun for us. We have enjoyed some wonderful trips and other special activities because early on we began to apply the Principle of the Four Quarters to the way we saved and handled our money.

We are not wealthy in the sense often applied to wealth by society. But we use that with which we have been blessed not only to meet our needs but also to meet other pressing needs in our community as well by investing in people and our experience confirms that such an investment pays large dividends. Frankly, in reviewing how we have used our money and other assets, I have come to the conclusion that wealth is not so much how much money one has but the attitude with which one uses his money and his other assets. In that sense, we would have to say that we do have some important wealth. Our use of our money and other assets has become for us a lifestyle that gives meaning and purpose to who we are. It is both a spiritual and a financial wealth that is not measured in dollars but in attitude.

TO HAVE OR NOT TO HAVE: MESSAGES SENT AND RECEIVED

OLIVER M. ROOPER

LIFE AS I REMEMBER IT began with a trauma. I was six years old when, on a Monday morning after an Easter Sunday, my mom came into my bedroom to wake me. I could tell by her bleary and red eyes she had been crying. I waited for the bad news. "I hate to tell you this, but Daddy died last night."

"What? After spending yesterday, Easter Sunday, at my uncle's farm hiding Easter eggs with my cousins and eating a wonderful meal? It can't be. This is not the way it is supposed to be. I'm only six. This is not right!" Those thoughts now at 77 years old still rumble through my mind like gathering storm clouds. The brain knows no time, so it was as if it were yesterday. It was yesterday. I remember the bedroom just as it was. The bed next to the windows which looked out on the front porch and at its edge, the blue hydrangeas that graced the summer days when I would romp through the woods to play with my friend Henry, only a half-block away. The chest of drawers against the wall next to the door. The short hallway that led to my parent's bedroom. A dresser with a mirror that stood in the corner of the room, the closet where my clothes were hung with order and care, a requirement of my mom's fastidious and rather compulsive nature.

My aunt Beth had arrived the night before, unannounced, simply saying that she had a premonition that something dreadful was about to happen to us. She boarded a train from Columbia, South Carolina, to Waycross, Georgia, and then a taxi, to arrive on our doorstep near my bedtime. Within an hour or so my daddy died. The doctor did come, but only in time to pronounce him dead. The diagnosis? A massive coronary.

Dad left us with a list of have-nots. He had built our house himself, but there was still a mortgage and a number of residual bills from the construction to be paid each month. Mom had only a high school education and no training or any skill that would support us. I was an only child, and she had counted on my dad being with us and providing the support, certainly needing help with an imaginative and bright six-year-old. From that spring day in April, the day of his death, to the end of my mom's life, it was a struggle for money, support, housing and the basics of life.

I was born in Jacksonville, Florida, and we lived there for several years while my dad worked at the post office. After his death, Mom went back to Jacksonville to work at the same post office and I stayed in Waycross with my aunt and uncle, Lila and B.J. Mom would come on the weekends to be with me. She finally gathered enough funds to bring me to Jacksonville. We lived in a rough section of town in one room and ate most of our meals off a hot plate in the room. It was a bare minimal life with no extras. No candy, no chewing gum, no treats of any kind. The landlady was struggling herself, and would charge us 50 cents in the winter to open the door to the hall where there was heat. We slept in a large feather bed, and on cold winter nights we sometimes had only our body heat to keep us warm. I looked forward to getting to school quickly so I could finally feel warm all over. I cursed Daddy a thousand times for abandoning us and dying before his time. There were two groups of youngsters my age that lived in the neighborhood. Today they would be called gangs, and though quite young, they were rough. Rock-throwing fights in the creek in front of our house were often and legendary. I was once struck in the head, knocked cold, and fell face first in the creek. A friend pulled me out before I drowned.

I still recall a fierce storm that filled the smelly creek to overflowing. My mom was at the post office and got off early because of the storm. The creek water had risen to within three steps of the porch, and the landlady and I were watching it with fear in our eyes. I remember looking down the road and watching Mom struggle against the swirling waters up to her waist while she held steadfastly to a rickety fence, pulling herself hand-over-hand until she reached our house. The hot plate meals, the small-time gangs, my several stitches, regular fights with the other "hoodlums," as Mom called them, the stinking creek, the rather consistent flooding of the same, all urged Mom to move in with relatives in a nicer subdivision in Jacksonville. We stayed in a small house nestled in the back room with Mom's sister's daughter and her husband and two children, both younger than I. We ate better than ever, and I still remember the great meals that Aunt Rain's daughter, Maggie, cooked for all of us. It was a labor of love. As a result, our current home for over 50 years has always been a place of refuge for those who needed some care, some hot meals, and a place to rest their heads. We have had dozens to be with us, some for a day, others for a month, a season, or longer. It seems that every race, color, creed, and station has had its feet under our table. It has been a grateful feeling, and one that goes back to that little house in Jacksonville, where we moved from near nothing to having a little more.

While we were in Jacksonville, Mom met a man, Stretch, dated him briefly, and ultimately married him. We moved to his place in Franklin, Indiana. He had a big two-story house, three grown children who also lived there, all on a 10-acre farm. It was there that I experienced my first snowfall, and with it the coldness of the human heart. This new husband and stepfather, Stretch, was not a happy man. Stern, austere, rigid, he took us to a fundamentalist church in the country. The preacher was one who employed the old hellfire and brimstone approach. He was frightening. I grew to hate Sundays. This new husband took out a hefty insurance policy on Mom, and a few months later, she woke me in the middle of the night. I knew that all Stretch's children had gone to sleepovers, and he had a three o'clock journey early that morning to do a carpentry job some miles away. Mom and I were alone in the house. When she woke me, I could smell the strong odor of gas. Mom immediately opened all the windows in the house and found the source of the smell. Stretch had turned on all the gas jets in the house, and he had obviously left us to die. Mom made a quick call to my aunt Beth in Columbia, South Carolina, and within an hour we packed several steamer trunks and suitcases, took two taxis to the train, and were on our way to Columbia. I was then about nine years old and again traumatized by this attempt on our lives.

We moved in with my aunt and her roommate, Karen, a bright but stern woman who owned the house and was totally bossy and domineering. Again, we were consigned to a small bedroom in the back of the house where we had virtually no privacy, the walls were paper thin, and if we wanted to have a private word with one another, it had to be a virtual whisper. To make matters worse, Karen had an ex-husband, an alcoholic, who would get totally inebriated and come banging on the front door in the middle of the night screaming that he was going to get in and kill us all. The police would come, arrest him, and there was generally no more sleep that night. That happened a number of times.

There was conflict between Mom and Karen, and we moved again to a place in Columbia on Green Street. It was an upstairs room, larger than any we had ever had, but it was cold and drafty with leaks in the roof. We ate out every night, and rain or shine we had to walk to the restaurant or cafeteria. The choices were limited, and eating the same every night, with peanut butter and jelly sandwiches in between, became laborious and tedious. My mom told me not to tell where we lived. We were both ashamed of the place. I remember that there was a church-sponsored dance that a girl invited me to, and I summoned the courage to go. After the dance, her father and mother were giving me a ride home and I made them let me out a block from the house so they would not see where I lived. They protested, but acquiesced. Shame was now a rather consistent part of my life, exacerbated by scarcity.

My aunt gave Mom a $5,000.00 loan for a down payment on a three-bedroom house in a new subdivision on Wheat Street in Columbia, just a block away from where my aunt lived. Finally, more room, privacy, a new place of our own, and some breathing space. But not for long. The aforementioned life had created within my mom a cadre of anxiety, which she took out on me. I could do nothing right. I was constantly scolded, beaten with a huge, hard rubber ironing cord, switches I had to pick for myself, and I was excoriated verbally every day for some minor infraction of her many rules and regulations.

We attended and joined the First Baptist Church in Columbia. Even there we were marginalized. Just about everyone there was moderately well off and we did not yet have a car and had to ride the bus to and from church. For any extra youth socials, we had to scrape together whatever additional monies were needed. Mom was working as a file clerk for the state, but the money was always a problem. More month than money to cover it all. Until I began working, it was a struggle.

The theology preached at our new church home seemed to be, "Wherever you are in life, it is God's will." I heard that at my dad's funeral, and it still made no sense. I heard that we were all the same in God's eyes, but that did not transfer to the economic and social realities that I faced. There was a gap in my mind about money and faith and the "blessings" that God bestowed. Some seemed significantly more blessed than others. Mom and I seemed to have drawn the short straw.

Another issue with money at the church was the tithe. It was preached incessantly as if we were robbing God if we did not tithe. But for my mom, to tithe compared to a rich man tithing comprised very different realities. His 90 percent remaining was greater than her 90 percent, since he had more to begin with. And anyway, if God was omnipotent, how could anyone rob God? It made no sense that someone could actually rob an omnipotent and omniscient God! If so, God was neither of those things! But the beat went on. One Sunday a month I heard a sermon on money and the tithe and a "stick 'em up robbery" to God, and the next was a sermon on alcohol and how awful it was. Then there was nearly always a sermon on being lost, going to hell, and getting saved from those licking flames, and one sermon that entailed an admonition on miscellaneous sins and misdeeds. No one seemed to mind this approach, and smiling faces greeted me each Sunday morning. Apparently, everyone seemed happy with the theology of the day, tithe and all.

I tell this story because it was teaching me volumes about having and not having. Not having was now, in my young mind, related to death, the struggle to live, living with relatives, getting only what was absolutely necessary for basic survival, being thrown in with unstable people like my stepfather whom I could not trust, moving in the middle of the night, fleeing for your life, living in back bedrooms with no privacy, depending on others for room and board, and being exposed to drunks and the rougher elements of life. Not having was now related to having a different name than your mother, and her being divorced in the 1940s, which made me the only kid in school whose parents were divorced. No fun and Mom's imposed anxiety seemed constant in my life. By my tenth year, I was anxious, shame-based, and beginning to form a vow that, with Scarlett O'Hara in *Gone With the Wind*, bore sentiments to the effect, "I will never be poor again. *Never, never, never*!

Money was always a problem and Mom's constant worry. She grieved and cried nights about not having enough, and she watched every penny. When I was thirteen, I lied about my age, got a paper route, financed through Mom a lawn mower from Sears Roebuck, and began to mow lawns in the summer. I also got her to buy me a bicycle on credit with the vow on my life that I would make the payments on the bike and the mower. I did pay them off and eventually bought our first television set the same way. Working now gave me money of my own, and I finally landed a second paper route, although at the time that was against the rules of the paper companies. Morning and evening were now taking me out of the house and away from the nagging and shaming to delivering my papers and making my own money. When Mom would get on one of her jags, I would walk the block to Aunt Beth's, and she would take me into her beautiful gardens and teach me about her flowers, and the beauty of gardening became my respite and therapy from the shaming I received at home. Aunt Beth was the most compassionate and loving person I have ever known. I still think I was born to the wrong sister! She was literally a lifesaver.

Mom wanted me to go to the University of South Carolina there in Columbia, but I knew inherently that she would sabotage my studies. I had to get away from her and reinvent myself without all the shame and anxiety she had instilled. I went to Furman University in Greenville, South Carolina. I did not have enough money for tuition, but the dean had compassion for me and gave me a work scholarship. For almost two years I worked in the cafeteria serving food. I proved myself academically and received a partial scholarship for that and landed a bass soloist scholarship with the Furman Singers. I also took a job as bass soloist for a local Baptist Church.

I met my future wife, Barbara, in the Singers. She was a Miss Greenville beauty who was also on voice scholarship as the soprano soloist for the Singers. We were married after graduation in August 1959, took a two-week honeymoon, and then headed off to Louisville, Kentucky, to the Southern Baptist Theological Seminary. Barbara taught school, and I studied hard, made great grades, and was an eager learner. My intellect caught fire at seminary, and I developed a passion for learning, a passion that is alive to this day. After the basic degree, I was invited to study for the master of theology degree, an academic degree that required a full thesis at that time. During my graduate study, I had a part-time country church in Owen County, Kentucky, mostly a farming community. The people were lovely and taught me much about life. They were more the teacher for me than I to them. I am, to this day, indebted to them for their love and grace toward the young preacher as they forgave my mistakes and educated me in such a gentle and caring way. I learned how to be a pastor from them. I was there for three years. I learned from these inspiring folk that although they did not have much, their generosity and giving were determined not by what they did not have but by what they had in their hearts.

After I completed my master's, I was invited to do a doctorate in theology. I began that, moved through three or four semesters of that degree when a larger, full-time church opened up in northern Kentucky that one of my professors wanted me to consider. I eventually took that church, and my doctorate was held open for me for five years. I fell in love with the pastoral ministry and never went back to complete the second graduate degree.

This first full-time church was, at that time, known in the community as the country club church. There were a few people in the congregation who were struggling, but most of the congregation was upper middle class to upper class, well educated, with considerable discretionary monies and a lifestyle that I had never seen. They gave me a membership at the country club so I could play golf with the members. I was, for the first time, introduced to a style of life that was shocking, satisfying, and reinforcing to that vow that not only would I never be poor again, but also I would strive for a life like I was witnessing at the church. Even more than that, I had a better education than many in the congregation, and I wanted and deserved what they had, and more. I began to desire what they had, dress like they did, enjoying the finer things, eat at the best restaurants, and since I had no discretionary funds like the members had, it was all on credit.

Then a funny thing happened. I found myself with not only a wife, but also now a first child, and I was scratching for money to pay off debts just like my mom years before. Good God. What had happened? It appeared that my vow never to be poor again had made me suddenly "money-poor" in spite of—no, because of—my vow. I overworked to gain favor with the congregation so they would give me more money and worked myself into a paralyzing clinical depression. I could not get out of bed. I took a leave of absence for a month, and a wonderful internist, fresh out of medical school, and who understood depression, brought me back to health with meds and conversation, and I continued on with my ministry at the church.

The unconscious seeds of ambition, envy, making myself "good enough," a fervent desire for finer things, were all taking root and growing into weeds in my spiritual life. My ability in the pulpit would be the magic carpet on which I would ride. "You are the best preacher in the entire area." It was consensus; everyone who heard me said so, therefore it must be true. I loved to hear it, and that drove me even more to keep up the reputation and to become even better. If I became better, I could go to bigger churches and get a better salary and benefits, and thus galvanize my family and myself from my ever-present dread of poverty and shame. I remembered: *never again*! I repressed that raw ambition with the justification that I was doing God's work and sacrificing a position in society that would have earned me ten times the salary. A number of established businessmen who were CEOs told me that. It must be gospel. None of this was truly and effectively conscious until years later as I went through more therapy and began a profoundly spiritual inventory with a Roman Catholic priest.

One of the insights I began to test at this first full-time church was that wealthy people might be wealthy because they find ways to keep their money. Some in the church were generous to a fault. But others were niggardly and seemed to take it personally if the church or I spent what they did not consider absolutely essential. Barbara and I lived in a parsonage, a house owned and maintained by the church. It seemed that those in charge of maintenance were always the tightest ones. If we had a repair problem, we sometimes had to wait to have repairs approved and then we had to accept the cheapest, and many times the least effective and least skilled repair solution accompanied by a handyman to do the work. It was false savings, but it looked frugal on the balance sheet that went to the church in conference and afforded kudos to the maintenance committee. Priorities mattered!

My half-conscious plan for rising in the ranks bore fruit, and one of the largest churches in the state called me to be its pastor. It was, at the time I went, a membership of 2,500 members. I found out later that the rolls were bloated and had not been purged for years. The search committee made many promises to get me, and among them were promises to lavishly furnish the two-story parsonage to our taste. Promises were one thing. But when the bills began to come in for the carpeting, the custom drapes, the custom paint job and all the other things we wanted, it all hit the fan, and the honeymoon was over quickly. The person we had to work with was obstinate and questioned every single thing we wanted, and we had to go "over his head" a number of times to fulfill the promises of the original committee. We did end up with a magnificent house that we opened constantly to the congregation for meetings, parties, groups, and a plethora of other occasions. Eventually I discovered the same thing in this church that I had found in the first one. Money was a huge issue and every dime had to be accounted for. Some folk were generous to a fault and others were niggardly as a fault.

While I was there, we established a weekday program for children, opened the gymnasium to the community youth, rented out the fifth floor of the educational building to Head Start and began a teen center in house next door that the church owned. We did this in conjunction with some Vista Volunteers who were working in the community. The principal progress, from my perspective, was that I led the church to dually align itself with a black Baptist Convention. This was 1969–70, when the racial issue was a hot topic. That project nearly cost me my pastorate, and only because the more progressive and younger couples came to support me was I able to stay. This led to another insight about money and the church and especially those who were wealthier. Many of them withheld their monies because of my progressive leadership. I will never forget the deacons' meeting in which the very conservative chair said: "I've got $1,500.00 in my drawer at home, and I won't give a dime of it until we sing some of the old songs and we stop some of these social programs. Pastor, what should I do with it?" The room was ensconced in a stony silence. "Go home, my brother, take it out of your drawer, give it to your wife, and tell her to go shopping! We will stay the course here!" Needless to say, that stirred up a hornet's nest of both opposition and support. I was able to stay there over seven years, and every one had seemingly endless money issues. When I left, I found crumpled in the back of my desk drawer, a half-dozen resignations, handwritten, but never sent. For years there were no raises, as if they were trying to starve me out, and we had to continuously borrow money. But by God's grace and Barbara's going back into teaching, we made it.

A group in the larger church came to me and asked that we withdraw from the church and form a house church and leave the constant conflict over doctrine, theology, and money. They were committed financially, and with their vowed support in every way, we did it. We became "The Church of the Redeemer," to be patterned after the Church of the Savior in Washington, DC. The church paid half my salary, and I became the alcohol coordinator at a mental health center in a nearby city. We were able to buy our first house with the help of the new church membership of about 25 members. We met in alternate houses every Sunday. I played the guitar, and we sang lustily, I preached, and we began to structure some mission projects. At our first meeting as a congregation to lay some infrastructure, I was called out of the meeting to answer a phone call from a search committee in a city near Washington, DC. I told them that I had just taken a church. They said I was their first choice out of some sixty candidates and if I changed my mind....

Almost a year later, I was exhausted from trying to be the pastor of the fledging church, writing a sermon, handling the counseling that they required, making any hospital calls that came up, and working to establish a transition house for alcoholics in my job. I was also working under an inept supervisor who was having trouble coordinating a staff of six when I had had been dealing with 16 staff members at the larger church. I called the professor who had recommended me to the church near DC, and asked him if that church had found a pastor. The answer was no and that he would call them and let them know I might be available. They called that night, and that weekend Barbara and I were on a plane to visit the church, just across the street from one of our nation's largest universities. They called me to be their pastor. Even though it was bittersweet to leave the house church, the members understood and were gracious to admit that despite it being a grand idea, it did not work, and they all needed to find themselves new congregations in which to serve.

I remained two years at this university church. They paid well, but we were again in a pastorium, and again it was like moving mountains to have repairs and any changes to the house made with dispatch. Most of the congregation was related to the university, and I could challenge their intellect and their hearts at the same time. They were more generous with their money for the most part, and only a couple of them were committed to grousing over the balance sheet every month. After the experience with the house, Barbara and I vowed that never again would we be at the whims of having our living space and its needs determined by a committee. The old saying was true: a camel was a horse put together by a committee. Again, the issue seemed to be how little money they could put into the house and still look frugal and discerning to the church in conference.

The church grew exponentially and soon there were people standing around the walls for the Sunday morning service. They wanted to build a new sanctuary. I knew a building program would mean that I would have to lead in raising money, and I did not want to do that. From my perspective it would take away from my spiritual life and my preaching as well. I delayed as long as I could. I sensed, correctly, that the church was going to build in spite of me, and I frankly did not know what to do but to acquiesce. By this time we had a second child and needed money in the worst way.

At that crucial time, a church in a huge metro area called me to see if I was interested in moving. They had just completed a new sanctuary and wanted a preacher who could expand the membership to fill up the new space. They had built a beautiful, well-conceived, liturgical space but did not have all the liturgics to go with it: no consistent historical liturgy in the worship service, no paraments, no stoles for the ministers, no consistent colors of the Christian year, no lectionary readings except for certain occasions, a communion rail but communion only once a quarter, and then not at the rail, no festival days, and a congregation that did not yet understand the worship space they had built.

The congregation had money. No, not every member, but the leadership was all leaders in business and in their community, and the money was there, although an oligarchy (rule by a few) decided the budget and where the money went. It was a beneficent oligarchy, but I learned quickly that those who gave the most had no compunction against wielding their financial power when it came down to it. I donned a Geneva preaching gown when I came. They were used to it, because the last minister had worn one when they moved into the new space. The word came from the wealthiest person in the congregation that if I wore that robe she would move her membership and come no more. I removed the robe with the proviso that within six months I would make the decision according to the feedback of the congregation. In six months, it was clear that the majority wanted me vested. I announced the decision, and I wore the vestments for 15 years. The people who made the threat liked the direction of new membership and the results of increased giving by the congregation, so they stayed.

We purchased our home near the church to complete the vow that we would no longer be prey to "maintenance by committee." It was a good feeling.

I learned many lessons from this congregation. There were no women on the finance committee. The men would gather at a restaurant on a Saturday morning, order breakfast, and plan the budget and financial expenditures that were needed. The trustees, who had access to certain specified monies, were on the finance committee most of the time, so there could be a mingling of funds if they decided to do so. It was an "old boys club," well-meaning and skilled, but I thought we needed a woman's voice for balance. I worked diligently for that purpose, and a woman who owned and was president of her own business was elected. Before this, when we met at the restaurant, no matter how good things were, there was always a perceived crisis and virtually every budget time there was a threat that we might have to cut staff. Almost half the budget would come in at the end of December, and it was nail biting time each year to see if we made the budget. Those with the money would watch carefully, and about the last day of December if there was a deficit, suddenly what we needed to make the budget would appear. It was always just short of a miracle. We all grew to expect it. I saw it as a way of controlling the church and its direction.

The impact that being in a wealthy congregation had on me personally and spiritually was incredible. I was rather awestruck when I saw how some of the wealthy lived. Their spacious and well appointed homes had the finest of everything. Their country club lifestyle, their discretionary monies to travel all over the world, their private schools for their children, their circle of influential and well-placed friends in powerful places, were all overt signs of the wealth they possessed. None of these folk bragged or were ostentatious with their money, but behind the scenes everyone knew who had the power when crucial decisions needed to be made within the church.

Unconsciously, I began to try to keep up with some of these moneyed folk. I went to the same men's store that the church leaders frequented, bought some of the same suits they did, and purchased cars that at least would not embarrass them when I parked in the senior minister's parking spot. When the money began to run out for us, we refinanced the house, and took some of the equity to try to keep up with our congregation. Spiritually, I knew that simplicity was really the life I should have had, but that old vow never to be poor again, never to be "under" to anyone was like a hidden disease gnawing at my spirit. It hid under the cover of providing the best for my family, giving them what everyone else had, giving them what I never had but wanted lustily. Soon I was well-placed in the community, on boards and in Rotary and on influential committees, more and more well-known for my preaching and speaking ability. I had to keep up the image and image costs, and so the house and its rapidly growing equity became our cash cow. Instead of going to one of these men or women in the congregation and asking their counsel for how to invest and grow a nest egg for the future, I unwisely competed with them. Money and its scarcity in my past and present began to command my spirit. In this one essential way at least, I was "not good enough."

All of this took a toll on me. The constant questioning if I was really good enough to be at this church gnawed at me. I never confessed this doubt to anyone, and I am sure that my confidence in the pulpit never revealed that I was nursing such a question. There were times when I asked myself, "What the hell am I doing here?" I knew, but I didn't know and was anything but certain, and living with that ambiguity and ambivalence was wearing on me consistently.

I was still in my early 40s when I had a terrible pain in my left arm one Thursday morning. I took a quick test walk, and before I had made it to the houses next door, I had to stop. I felt I was about to have a heart attack. I called my doctor, he saw me immediately, put me on some meds, did tests, and within a few days I was in the hospital ready for my first two bypasses with a 90 percent blockage to several crucial vessels. To complicate matters, my associate, who was to preach for me while I recovered, was discovered having an affair with a woman in the church, and that affair broke open while I was getting ready for surgery. "No stress," said the doc. Good luck with that! The congregation rallied around the family and me and was incredibly understanding. I recovered and went on to stay for a full fifteen years.

At a morning breakfast, one of the wealthier men in the congregation told me that he and a few others thought it was time for me to leave the church as the pastor. He could give me no reason why, it was just time. I have always resisted someone trying to force me to do something. Against his wishes, I talked to the majority of the leadership about this man's proposal. Most thought I was not finished at the church and were upset that this man was trying to force me to leave. This is not unusual in Southern Baptist churches, but after 15 years I felt it was a bit odd that the oligarchy wished to handle it this way. But as the wife of this man once told me: "Those with the gold make the decisions!" Money came into play even more obviously, when, to force the issue even further, the man and his family pulled out their money and withheld it. In fact, the man himself took money that he had already given and withdrew it, which many thought illegal, but because he was a huge supporter of the church, no one wanted to cross him.

It was at that time that I decided with Barbara that a move we had been talking about for a couple of years had matured. I resigned to enter the Episcopal Church and to begin the process for priesthood. I understand this was a shock for many, but some had said that our church was more Episcopal than many Episcopal churches in the metro area.

The bishop called me while I was in the process for priesthood and asked me to take over the directorship of a program for men recovering from substance abuse, a ministry that had strong ties to the diocese. It was virtually bankrupt, and the last director had allegedly stolen some money from the program. I took that position, helped to right the ship, brought on a new board, bought four houses for the recovering men, paid off the loans, renovated the houses, and left the organization strong and ready for the next director. During my tenure as head of this transition ministry, the bishop called again and wanted me to go to a small church in the diocese and help re-establish it. A priest had virtually decimated the church with bad behavior. I went to this church as the bishop's vicar and for three years assisted them in their successful attempt to bring the church to good order.

I was in school, head of the transition ministry, vicar at the church, maintaining two offices for my psychotherapy practice, and moving through a difficult process toward priesthood. All this proved to be too much. I suffered a massive heart attack in the parking lot of a local hospital and had immediate surgery that resulted in five more bypasses to join the other two I had had in 1979. A month later I walked down the aisle of the cathedral and was ordained an Episcopal priest. After four short years in the church as a priest I was chosen as the canon pastor of the Episcopal cathedral in the diocese of this metro area. Even with five to six thousand members, there were money issues. I relearned a lesson that I had experienced at other churches. The majority will let the wealthier give for them unless greater awareness becomes theirs. This congregation had people from every walk of life. The poor who needed constant support, the middle class, the wealthy, all there for their own reasons and motivations. Some were generous and loving, full of gratitude for what life had brought them. Others were, like in every congregation, grasping and conserving so much so that giving seemed painful to them. What has troubled me the most in virtually all the churches in which I served has been the issue of members who willfully use their resources in an attempt to control and manipulate events and directions for the majority in the congregation.

While at this cathedral, a psychiatrist, several others, and I formed a counseling and spiritual life center, the first in the 147-year history of the cathedral. The cathedral was helpful with a loan for the center, a move for which I am grateful. They later forgave the loan. A power struggle ensued in the years to come, and the center separated from the cathedral and eventually came to bear my name. We had a good run of some 14 years. The center is no longer in existence for reasons too numerous to mention here. But huge amounts of money were raised over those years, and I found people who were so very generous and caring, good stewards of their resources and without them the center would not have existed. Their thousands of dollars helped multitudes of clients whose names the donors will never know. I still receive reminders from those who walked through our doors: "You and this center saved my life!" All the pieces of the larger puzzle fall into their proper places with those words. I, we—now they—have made and are making a redeeming difference.

Conclusion: There are many other facets of my life that space in this essay will not permit me to present. I have left out details and have given emphasis to the events that highlight the general theme of these essays. This approach might leave the reader with many questions. I still have many myself.

What I have described is my life and the varied experiences I have had with money, scarcity, events in the churches I have had (seven in all), and some of their experiences with abundance, discretionary monies, using money to control, and using money to bless and help those who need it most. For me, the early experiences of not having and their myriad consequences certainly colored the way I saw life and its scarcity/abundance for a long time. Even into my 77th year, I still smart when I think how different it might have been had my dad lived and abated the anxiety of my obsessive and abusive mom. My mom did teach me perseverance, namely, that we do not give up no matter what, and for that I am so very grateful. Otherwise, I think I would have left the ministry long ago.

My story is not finished. I am still in ministry, now as a psychotherapist in private practice, and I see the devastating affects that having money and not having money, and the resources it provides, can have on a person's entire outlook on life. Struggle is not all bad. In fact one of the great lessons of life that I have experienced is that there is bane and blessing in virtually everything. Am I bitter now as I contemplate the last few years of my life? Not at all. Through therapy, reflection, meditation, and prayer, I have learned to see that even in the scarcest of times, there was blessing, and in the best of times, trial and temptation. I cannot change the past, but I can interpret it in such a way that emphasizes the blessings and puts the pain and struggle in proper perspective.

TWIN LEGACIES

DONNA S. MOTE

I AM THE GRANDCHILD OF *sharecroppers*. I know that now at age fifty. It has been the truth and been part of my life since before I was born. Until I was in my forties, however, it was a truth that was obscured either intentionally by avoiding it—or at least avoiding the naming of it—or simply left opaque.

The clues came to me in little pieces of information through the years. When we would travel each October and at other times to the town around which my father spent most of his childhood and all his teenaged years until he entered the workforce full-time, Dad would point to a number of places along the way and say, "And we lived there one while."

My mother would remark that my paternal grandfather "never kept a job for very long." Through the years I overheard comments about my grandfather "having a temper" and being "bad to drink." I learned a laundry list of jobs that Papa Mote worked at in his short but hard fifty years. I learned the locations of many of the tenant houses my father, his brothers, and his parents occupied, along with my father's paternal grandfather in his blind and widowed dotage, and the fields my grandparents were responsible for cultivating on shares.

The more I learned about my father's childhood, the tenuousness of home for him when he was growing up, the necessity of paid work from him from first grade on, the more I understood why it was so important to him that my siblings and I have a house from which we never had to move. The house Dad built for us was never mortgaged because my Dad built it in stages, paying cash as he went for all the materials and doing the construction himself.

The more I learned about the harsh economic realities of my father's formative years, the more I understood what he meant when he said, "I wanted my children to have more than I did."

I am the grandchild of *landowners*. I have known that since early childhood. My mother was born in the house where her father was also born, the house her father's parents had built in stages beginning with the year of their marriage in 1865.

The house my mother grew up in was just down the road from the first house built by the Elliotts in that county in 1825. She is a fifth-generation native of the county on her father's side and a sixth-generation native on her mother's side.

My parents were born in 1920 and 1924, respectively. They endured the Great Depression as children. Those years were not pleasant for either of their families, but my mother's experience of stability contrasted starkly with my father's experience of instability and the reality of greater privation connected with it. The common experience of the Great Depression was not enough to bridge the divide between the pride—and relative safety—of property ownership and the shame—and relative danger—of its lack.

My father carried what I now understand as shame about his family's instability, his father's alcoholism, and the circumstances of his upbringing until his death at age ninety in 2010. That was part of why he talked so little about his people or his places. My mother, conversely, even now at age ninety celebrates daily her many connections to family near and far as a person who has people.

I am the grandchild of all four of my grandparents and the child of both my parents. These twin legacies, these different streams find their confluence in me and in my views of property, ownership, finance, stewardship, and money.

My dad's experience makes me wary of romanticizing poverty that is not chosen, for example, monastic poverty or a radically simplified off-the-grid lifestyle observed out of a commitment to particular ethical and environmental values. Because of what my father had no choice about as a child, I know that opting to be poor is the prerogative of privilege.

My mom's experience makes me value connection to land, to a particular place over the long haul through successive generations. It has helped me understand property ownership as stewardship of a particular patch of the planet although I chafed against the idea of property ownership in a capitalist society as a young person fresh out of seminary and keen to be highly mobile.

The house my dad built for us is situated halfway between the home place where my mother and her father grew up and the home place where my mother's mother grew up. It is multiple counties away from the numerous places my father bounced around to in his formative years. The house my dad built for us on land my parents purchased from my mom's family is the only house I ever lived in until I went off to college. When my mom dies, I will inherit the house and its adjacent property. I already have stewardship over many aspects of the care of my home place, both house and grounds.

My parents, once they began building what would be my home place, never had a mortgage, and they never had any other debt. They paid cash for cars and other big-ticket items following a pay as you go plan that was made possible both by their frugal choices and the unprecedented—and unrepeatable—rising economic tide in the post-World War II era.

 I received a full scholarship and had no debt whatsoever when I completed my undergraduate degree as a first-generation college student. I went straight on to seminary and, even though I had debt when I graduated, I had paid it all off within twelve years of graduating. Then I began a long-anticipated doctoral program. I received a great deal of scholarship and stipendiary support from my university, but I took out large student loans as well, taken aback by the astonishing increases in tuition and fees in the fourteen years between completing my master's and beginning my doctorate.

 I now serve in a ministry position I proposed and co-created in partnership with my bishop. I reap rich dividends spiritually, emotionally, and personally on a daily basis. I also struggle with paying off my educational debt while helping to pay off a mortgage on the house in which I now live.

 I live thirty miles from my home place and experience the joy of spending time with my mom, who proudly and determinedly lives there alone in her blind and widowed dotage along with the stretch and crush of competing time demands upon me as I live in this season in the "sandwich generation" caring for elders and children alike.

 In midlife I once again recognize my parents' wisdom to live debt-free even as I acknowledge that I will be in significant debt for several more years. Attending to debt retirement while at my current level of cash compensation drastically undercuts my ability to save for retirement as I would like. My goal is to retire debt-free to that never-mortgaged home my parents built and continue the stewardship of the land that is my inheritance on my mother's side for nearly 200 years and the stewardship of the house whose debt-free construction broke the cycle of instability on my father's side.

 I am the grandchild of sharecroppers. I am the grandchild of landowners. These twin legacies, these different streams find their confluence in me and in my views of property, ownership, finance, stewardship, and money.

THE WAR ON POVERTY:
A YOUNG BAPTIST'S EXPERIENCE

BILL J. LEONARD

IN THE YEAR THAT Martin Luther King and Robert Kennedy were assassinated, I worked for the War on Poverty in Dallas County, Texas. It was 1968: the summer after I graduated from Texas Wesleyan and took my army physical as demanded by the Selective Service Administration, the summer that I became engaged to be married—momentous moments to say the least. Actually, I worked for two summers, 1968 and 1969, in the Community Action Program of Dallas' War on Poverty. I can't remember how I got the job, but I sought it when the Baptist Church where I was youth minister was unable to pay me full time. The first summer I ran a recreation program in Balch Springs, Texas, a predominately Caucasian community. The next summer, 1969, I was a "coordinator" of three Dallas county programs, one in the predominately white town of Wilmer, another in the Carver Heights section of Dallas, and another in Lancaster, Texas, just outside Dallas. The latter two were in African American communities. Today I'm still convinced that working in the War on Poverty changed my life.

The War on Poverty was a massive government program set in motion fifty years ago as one of many legislative initiatives in President Lyndon Johnson's Great Society agenda, and included the Civil Rights Act (1964), the Voting Rights Act (1965), as well as Medicaid, Head Start, and student loan programs. In 2014, the fiftieth anniversary of the founding of the Civil Rights Act, the five living US presidents participated in ceremonies celebrating the half-century anniversary of its passage.

Critics then and now charge that the anti-poverty "war" fostered a dependence on the government "dole," an initiative-crushing affliction created by the American "welfare state," and a well-intended project that ended in ultimate failure. Others acknowledge its limitations amid efforts to respond to life-destroying poverty in the world's richest nation. In her master's thesis at the University of North Texas entitled "Dallas, Poverty, and Race: Community Action Programs in the War on Poverty" (2008), Harriet DeAnn Rose wrote, "Although the War on Poverty had minimal economic success, the poverty programs did reach people." She cited Dallas community leader Willis Johnson's insistence that the poverty program was not a "handout," but a "hand up," and concluded that it

> helped the poor to realize that they were no longer an invisible entity within the nation but could make a difference in the politics of the city and the lives of their families, a legacy that lives on today.

In an article in *The Rural Blog*, Tim Mandell reflects on the impact of the War on Poverty fifty years from its founding, noting that it aided in dropping the poverty rate from 24 percent in 1960 to 14.3 percent in 2012. Mandell concludes that government programs were more effective in reducing poverty than previously thought. In *Uneven Ground: Appalachia Since 1945*, Appalachian scholar Ronald Eller writes extensively about the war on poverty as centered in Appalachia. Though critiquing the liberal social strategies that often stereotyped impoverished people, Eller writes, "For Appalachia, the war on poverty was as much an attitude, a moral crusade, as a set of programs," that created "a core group of young poverty warriors" whose "commitment to social justice and reform" evolved beyond the war on poverty itself.

I can't claim that those two summer experiences made me a very formidable "young poverty warrior," but it transformed my thinking and acting in the world in profound ways. Indeed, the pastor of the church where I was youth minister fretted that the War on Poverty was "making a liberal" out of me on issues of race, economics, and social engagement that would distance me from Southern Baptists. I guess he was right. In 1968–69 it did seem radical. For one thing, all my supervisors, my bosses, were African Americans, meaning that I was probably among the first white people ever to work for black people in Dallas County, Texas. Having mentors, even for two brief summers, who knew about poverty and racial disparity first hand, was a life-shaping learning experience.

Mentors were everywhere in those two summers. As a "coordinator" of three programs in 1969 I worked with three women who ran those respective programs, another amazing learning experience. The first time I showed up at the Lancaster, Texas community center the Pentecostal African American director said: "Son, we'd hoped they'd hire our [meaning African American] young people as coordinator, but since they hired you we'll just have to learn to work together." From that moment on she nurtured me into that African American setting, the most intense racial engagement I had encountered up to that time. Together we organized recreational programs, field trips (including a day at Six Flags when it was over 110°—I haven't cooled down yet), and work projects, using much of the budget to construct a basketball court that lasted for years. On my last day she gave me a wedding present and said: "Son, turned out you did us good." I've never received a more gracious, albeit undeserved, benediction.

Efforts to respond to poverty in the United States are as old as the Republic itself, often creating divisions even among the church's most orthodox adherents. "Poor relief" was a standard procedure for aiding the impoverished, a practice brought from European churches. It involved churchly efforts to respond to the poor through special offerings, direct food aid, and other benevolent actions. By the nineteenth century, home mission societies were coordinating many of these endeavors. Later on, "settlement houses" became centers for developing training programs, food and housing efforts, and even an attempt to offer "the poor" help with varying degrees of dignity. In *The Religious Mission of the Irish People and Catholic Colonization*, Roman Catholic bishop John Lancaster Spalding described the state of urban poverty in America. He wrote:

> Now, the poor in our great cities and manufacturing towns have no homes. They live in tenements and hired rooms; or if the more fortunate own their cottages they can have little hope of leaving them to their children, who will go to swell the great floating population that is up for universal hire, and which, work failing, sinks lower to join the army of paupers and outcasts who form, to use the modern phrase, the dangerous classes of our great commercial and manufacturing centers.

By the late 19th century, however, divisions were clearly evident in Protestant communities over the meaning of poverty and the church's response to it. In an 1889 treatise entitled *The Gospel of Wealth*, Christian industrialist Andrew Carnegie wrote:

> The problem of our age is the administration of wealth, so that the ties of brotherhood may still bind together the rich and poor in harmonious relationship.... The contrast between the palace of the millionaire and the cottage of the laborer with us today measures the change that has come with civilization. This change, however, is not to be deplored, but welcomed as highly beneficial.

The Gospel of Wealth introduced Carnegie's plan for using vast financial resources accumulated by certain individuals at the height of the Industrial Revolution. The phrase, Gospel of Wealth, came to characterize the approach of certain 19th century Protestants, centered in a type of socioeconomic Darwinism suggesting that some people were "elected" to accumulate money. Carnegie sought to channel this economic theory into philanthropic practice. He wrote:

> It is well, nay, essential for the progress of the race, that the houses of some should be homes for all that is highest and best in literature and the arts, and . . . the refinements of civilization. . . . Much better this great irregularity than universal squalor. . . . We start, then, with a condition of affairs under which the best interests of the race are promoted, but which inevitably gives wealth to the few. Thus far, accepting conditions as they exist, the situation can be surveyed and pronounced good.

Carnegie accepted this economic condition as a social and theological given, and insisted that the "only question" was, "What is the proper mode of administering wealth after the laws upon which civilization is founded have thrown it into the hands of the few?" He then outlined ways that the wealthy could use a portion of their funds to benefit society.

Carnegie was not alone. In *Acres of Diamonds*, a widely circulated address published in 1890, Baptist pastor Russell Conwell encouraged the accumulation and proper use of wealth. Of the poor, Conwell commented:

> Some men say, "Don't you sympathize with the poor people?" Of course I do. . . . I won't give in but what I sympathize with the poor, but the number of poor who are to be with is very small. To sympathize with a man whom God has punished for his sins, thus to help him when God would still continue a just punishment, is to do wrong, no doubt about it, and we do that more than we help

those who are deserving. While we should sympathize with God's poor-that is, those who cannot help themselves-let us remember that is not a poor person in the United States who was not made poor by his own shortcomings, or by the shortcomings of someone else. It is all wrong to be poor, anyhow. Let us give in to that argument and pass that to one side.

Many late 19th century preachers equated poverty with divine retribution. In the 1870s, Henry Ward Beecher, pastor of Plymouth Congregational Church, Brooklyn, insisted that no man in this land suffers from poverty unless it be more than his fault—unless it be his sin.

The Social Gospel and Catholic Worker movements challenged those ideas, calling American Christians to reclaim Jesus' own continued engagement with and concern for the poor. Social Gospel advocate Walter Rauschenbusch saw poverty firsthand as pastor in Hell's Kitchen, New York, through "an endless procession" of families "out of work, out of clothes, out of shoes, and out of hope." Rauschenbusch called for the conversion of sinners and of corporations that exploited them. Although the crassness of those 19th century preachers now seems less public, our 21st century sentiments sometime betray an implicit belief that those in poverty are "moochers" or "welfare cheaters." Even though abuse of private/public programs does occur, the facts suggest the rapid growth of poverty in our day.

While certainly not limited to Baptists, the Social Gospel was formed by numerous Baptist individuals including Rauschenbusch, sometimes known as the father of the movement. Born into a German Baptist home in 1886, Rauschenbusch was educated in Germany and at Rochester Theological Seminary. Entering the ministry, he served eleven years as pastor of a German Baptist church in Hell's Kitchen, an area plagued by serious social problems. He then became professor of church history at Rochester Seminary and wrote extensively on the nature of the Social Gospel. In 1893, he became one of the founders of an organization known as the Brotherhood of the Kingdom, a group seeking to carry out Jesus' teaching in both church and society. In affirming the immediacy of God's kingdom, Rauschenbusch offered his own critique of American political and economic exploitation of workers and the impoverished. In *Christianity and the Social Crisis* (1907) he wrote: "Our cities are poor, unclean, always laying heavy burdens of taxation on the producing classes." It was a "deep-rooted injustice." He lamented that workers were paid "fixed wages," noting,

> The upward movement of this wage is limited by the productiveness of his work; the downward movement of it is limited only by the willingness of the workman to work at so low a return.

Committed to the conversion of individuals to Christian faith, Rauschenbusch was equally concerned for the transformation of society through the rule and reign of God in the world.

So however the statisticians and politicians may evaluate the War on Poverty, I can say that I observed, indeed experienced, its economic and racial benefits during two brief summers in a volatile Texas county where race and economic divisions still abound. I saw people work together in places where segregation of race, class, and culture had long kept them apart. I watched some young people have some experiences and opportunities they had never had before. The lessons mentored into me by a Pentecostal African American woman haunt me half century later: For church and nation, in the war on poverty there can be no truce.

Portions of this essay were originally published by Associated Baptist Press, "Can I Get a Witness," April 10, 2014, *The War on Poverty: A Young Baptist's Experience*.

WHAT WOULD I HAVE TO SAY ABOUT WEALTH IF I WAS WARREN BUFFETT'S PASTOR?

LOU SNEAD

IT SEEMS TO ME that conversations about money and wealth are often difficult subjects for many of us to address. Issues around personal incomes and finances are very private matters for most of us. Asking about someone's personal wealth is considered to be rude, intrusive, and impolite. Surveys also tell us that many people with six figure annual incomes who live in gated, country club communities and own several pieces of real estate, drive expensive cars, and have accumulated wealth and investments with no significant debt still do not consider themselves to be rich. Having served as a pastor of affluent churches in both Dallas and Houston, I have found this to be true. In the minds of many successful and affluent church people I have encountered, the "wealthy" are represented by billionaires like Bill Gates and Warren Buffett, or those with family fortunes like the Waltons and Rockefellers, and highly paid athletes and movie stars. So, the very definition of "wealth" is a relative term when it comes to household incomes or bank balances and how much net worth someone has to have in order to be considered to be among the "wealthy." Even though we Americans are on the whole the wealthiest people on the planet, we often do not see ourselves as being "wealthy" as individuals because we tend to reserve that designation just for the superrich.

In my thirty-five years of ministry, I have found that conversations about money and wealth are particularly difficult matters for many ministers and church members to have with one another. There is a host of dynamics involved whenever the issue of wealth or money comes up in church circles. Ministers sometimes struggle with offending and placating their wealthy church members whenever we broach the subject of wealth within the Christian life. When addressing the issue of money and wealth we can easily get caught between the desire to be both pastoral and prophetic. Despite any notion that the gospel calls us to "comfort the afflicted and to afflict the comfortable," about the only time we attempt to preach about money is during the annual stewardship season or when the church embarks on a capital campaign. We get that parishioners understand the institutional realities about money. Even when we address the church's need for financial support we try not to sound too pointed or too self-serving in our asking for financial commitments from our congregations. Since most ministers go into the ministry out of a higher calling to serve the gospel, it's not unusual for church members to assume that church professionals are not working just for money or to get rich. Consequently, churches are often among some of the lowest paying institutions in America. I have found that some pastors, like myself, are reluctant to know how much money our members contribute to the church. We worry that such information might unwittingly influence how we relate to our wealthy members or how this knowledge might turn into resentments towards the wealthy that are stingy. Money issues get even more complicated by the fact that many church folk get down-right apoplectic over the issue of confidentiality when it comes to who gives how much to the church. So for a litany of reasons, ministers and church members alike become anxious and ambivalent when any attempt is made to address the subject of wealth within the Christian context.

I believe that some of our ecclesiastical reluctance to talk about wealth also grows out of the mixed messages about money that are imbedded in the biblical narratives and in our faith traditions. On the one hand, I am struck by the number of poignant biblical passages that suggest that money and wealth can separate us from the love of God and from loving our neighbors. Jesus warns that we cannot worship both God and mammon (riches). In Mark's gospel, Jesus notes that it is hard for those who trust in their riches to enter the kingdom of God. The Apostle Paul suggests that the love of money is the root of all evil. Money and wealth are often portrayed in the New Testament as dangerous spiritual contaminates. Early on, the Roman Catholic Church insisted that its priests take a vow of poverty in order to avoid the temptations of materialism in service to God.

On the other hand, I also know that there are biblical stories and teachings that imply that money and wealth are not intrinsically evil in themselves. In the Genesis narrative, God is said to be the provider of riches for Abraham and his descendants. The Wisdom writer speaks favorably about those who save some of their abundance for the future. According to Matthew 25:14–30, wealth is a gift from God that is to be used in service to those in need. In his story about the unjust steward, Jesus seems to encourage sucking up to the wealthy: "I tell you, use worldly wealth to gain friends for yourselves, so that when it is gone, you will be welcomed into eternal dwellings" (Luke 16:9). Paul instructs the leaders of the early church to

> command those who are rich in this present world not to be arrogant nor put their hope in wealth, which is uncertain, but to put their hope in God, who richly provides us with everything for our enjoyment (1 Timothy 6:17–19).

I have even preached stewardship sermons that suggested God doesn't need our money, only our gratitude, citing an Old Testament passage saying that when making an offering to God is too difficult it is appropriate to spend the money on whatever you wish- food, wine, sheep, etc.- and have a party to rejoice in our blessings (Gen 14:22–26).

Rather than offering a wholesale condemnation of wealth, I find some New Testament texts suggesting that it's the desire to have riches, combined with the temptations and greed that wealth can bring, along with the self-assurances of wealth itself that actually corrupt us spiritually and socially, e.g., 1 John 3:17. The 17th century evangelist, John Wesley, preached a favorable view of wealth, claiming that the Bible teaches us to "earn all the money you can, save all the money you can, and give all the money you can." Some contemporary evangelists today embrace and preach a "gospel of prosperity" saying that scripture teaches that God intends to bless us not only spiritually but materially as well. So, rather than being hostile towards wealth or those who are rich, it's easy to find a long strand within the Christian tradition that supports the spirit of capitalism and sees the accumulation of wealth as a gift from God. Even though the "prosperity gospel" sounds terribly self-serving to me and a one-sided reading of scripture, I recognize that some preachers have found biblical justification for this endorsement of accumulated wealth and many people are attracted to this version of the gospel. Oddly enough, this doesn't seem to appeal to many of those who are very wealthy.

As a pastor I have found that my attempts to talk about wealth and money in the church today are further complicated by the economic and consumerist culture we live in here at the beginning of the 21st Century. In some real respects, the devotion to money has eclipsed a faith in God in the heart and minds of most Americans. The health of our economy dominates both our national and our personal sense of security. As Walter Brueggemann has pointed out, we live as people of faith within a culture that believes in the "myth of scarcity" more than the "liturgy of abundance" that the biblical witness asks us to embrace. When it comes to our pocketbooks, it's amazing how conservative we all become, because we have bought into the cultural notion about scarcity of our resources in relation to the abundance of our resources.

In most cultures, and particularly in our own, achieving a measure of wealth equates to having power, not only in the marketplace, but in social status, political influence, and personal freedom. Despite the fact that I am convinced that wealth never in itself brings happiness, it does ward off the kind of anxieties and struggles that poverty entails. Most of us who claim to be people of faith can certainly appreciate the kind of security, freedom, and independence that some measure of wealth can bestow on us. So I don't try to spiritualize away the fact that we live in the world where wealth is associated with economic, social, and political power and disproportionate opportunities to succeed in life. In my own ministry with upper-middle class congregations, I have found that it is spiritually pointless and arrogant to suggest that having wealth is in itself an evil condition or that money is somehow dirty. For me, the generosity of some wealthy people and the good that can be done with money contradict this old bias that the Church has held at times. I hope that I can be spiritually sophisticated enough to realize that money is in itself morally neutral. From my experience, it is more often our addiction to money and what money can buy that produces harm. Since power from wealth can have a corrupting effect on any of us, this is often the moral blind side that can come from having great wealth.

Trying to preach prophetically about wealth in our culture today, however, does present some real challenges and even resistance. I have learned to my chagrin that those in the Church who are opposed to mixing religion with politics don't like the suggestion that people of wealth easily control our political institutions. Likewise, I have found that those who have wealth sometimes have difficulty acknowledging that their wealth gives them an advantage over middle-class and low-income families whether socially, educationally, or economically in terms of generating even more wealth and adding to the growing divide between the rich and poor. Too often there is an attitude among the prosperous in our culture that says, "I earned my wealth and others have had the same opportunity to earn theirs," so it's only the difference in work ethic that separates the haves from the have-nots. I have found in my ministry that there is actually resistance among not only many wealthy people but also among middle-class folk to talk about economic justice out of fear that we might mess up the invisible hand of free-market capitalism that has produced a lot of wealth for some and less wealth for others. I am always amazed how often discussions about economic inequities today will provoke those who are the beneficiaries of marketplace capitalism to blame the poor for their inability to become self-sufficient and economically successful. Moreover, the defensiveness among the wealthy often ignores that some economists now tell us when the disparity between rich and poor becomes too wide, as in the case of the one percent vs. 99 percent of today, free market capitalism actually suffers and some form of redistribution of wealth needs to occur (see Joseph Stiglitz, *The Price of Inequality: How Today's Divided Society Endangers Our Future*, 2013).

So, given all these dynamics, I have struggled at times with the issue of how much pastoral sensitivity I should have and what I should encourage church members to exercise towards material wealth. It's fairly easy to suggest that Christians should avoid envy, philandering, or disdain toward the wealthy among us. For those who worked hard for their fortunes, it is generally easy for me to offer respect and to give them a blessing. Admittedly, I find it more difficult to be pastoral toward those who seem to believe their wealth should give them special privileges, honor, or disproportionate power in our collective living.

My experience as a pastor has taught me that it is important for pastors to acknowledge that not all wealthy people are greedy, opportunistic, stingy, or insensitive to the moral/social responsibilities that accompany their wealth. Over the years, I have been surprised to discover that some of my wealthiest parishioners felt guilty at times about their prosperity or taken for granted in terms of their congregational giving. I have been touched at times by the level of generosity that I have seen from people of both modest and significant wealth when they heard stories of people struggling with issues of poverty or unexpected financial disasters. From these experiences I have found that wealthy church members often want and need pastoral care that recognizes both the burden and the opportunities that their wealth provides to them.

In some ways very wealthy people are no different from those of us who have only a relatively small amount of wealth. Most of us respond appreciatively to the call for gratitude for the blessings of life we have been given. Most of us resonate with examples of people living out of generosity rather than out of fear or greed. Most of us feel affirmed when we can use our resources, whether great or small, to help others in need or to provide for the common good. The most effective sermon on wealth I ever heard was preached by the daughter of a small town grocery store owner who provided college tuition money and books for some of the young people who had worked in his store over the years. I remember her telling us that her family knew that her father had kept in touch with the parade of young people who worked in his store as clerks, stock boys, or grocery deliverers after they graduated from high school and left town. "What we didn't know," she said,

> until Daddy died, was the amount of money that he had sent to a number of those over the years who couldn't afford to go to college on their own. We only discovered his secret generosity when Mother found a stack of thank-you letters from those he had helped that he had kept locked in his desk drawer.

She concluded her sermon by saying how much her father's quiet generosity had shaped her own sense of gratitude for all that she had been given and had actually inspired her to go into the ministry because her father learned this attitude about giving from reading the Bible and going to church.

Most pastors, of course, will never have the opportunity to serve a church where super-rich people like Warren Buffett could be among their membership. But, if I had such an opportunity, I often wonder what I might have to say to those who have enormous wealth. Sometimes it is best for honest conversations about money to take place among our peers. Andrew Carnegie, the Scottish American industrialist who led the enormous expansion of the American steel industry of the late 19th century, was also one of the highest profile philanthropists of his era. By the time he died, he had given away almost 90 percent of his accumulated wealth to charities and foundations, amounting to, in 1919, $350 million; whereas, in 2014, this would be $4.76 billion! From his own faith background, Carnegie wrote an article in 1889 entitled "The Gospel of Wealth," wherein he called on the rich of his day to use their wealth to improve society. In this article Carnegie suggested there are only three ways of dealing with great wealth: leaving it as inheritance to family, which he thought was the poorest way of handling wealth; bequeathing it for public good; and supporting projects and institutions that strengthen the common good and the hand of poor (education, work opportunities, the arts, etc.) but that do not harm the principle of private property, the law of competition, or the accumulation of wealth. He stated,

> This, then, is held to be the duty of the man of Wealth: First, to set an example of modest, unostentatious living, shunning display or extravagance; to provide moderately for the legitimate wants of those dependent upon him; and after doing so to consider all surplus revenues which come to him simply as trust funds, which he is called upon to administer, and strictly bound as a matter of duty to administer in the manner which, in his judgment, is best calculated to produce the most beneficial results for the community— the man of wealth thus becoming the mere agent and trustee for his poorer brethren, bringing to their service his superior wisdom, experience and ability to administer, doing for them better than they would or could do for themselves.

Carnegie's own encouragement about managing wealth, in turn, stimulated a wave of philanthropy among the wealthy of his era producing some of the best examples of improving the common good that this country has ever seen. Carnegie's reflection on his own wealth leads me to think that the best we can do for the wealthy is to encourage them to have conversations with their peers about the spiritual and moral burden and responsibilities that their wealth gives to them.

Second, I have learned that people of faith who are willing to acknowledge our material and economic blessings can readily recognize and own together the temptations and problems that grow out of our consumerist culture. One of the legitimate functions of our faith traditions, it seems to me, is to mitigate against the excesses and abuse of wealth and the power that often plague the rich. Some of the most honest and engaging conversations about wealth and money that I have had with my parishioners came out of Christian education classes developed around the film series and book about the disease of "affluence" that afflicts so many of us today who are even moderately wealthy. I have also found a strong willingness to address the benefits and challenges of wealth when our church offered book studies and discussion groups that address personal and cultural economic issues and concerns—e.g., books like *Luxury Fever* by Robert Frank, *Your Money Or Your Life* by Joe Dominguez and Vicki Robin, and *God The Economist* by M. Douglas Meeks. In terms of my own edification about living with wealth in a world filled with poverty, the best conversations I can remember having occurred when a group of us pastors read and discussed together a theological paper produced by our Presbyterian denomination entitled "Christian Faith and Economic Justice."

If I pastored a church today with many wealthy people, I would be eager to explore together within the congregation what the gospel suggests to us about our material riches and how we manage our money. So I suspect that my convictions about wealth and money would make a lot of people feel awkward and nervous if I served a church where Warren Buffett was a member.

CONTRIBUTORS

CATHY ABBOTT is the Arlington District Superintendent, Virginia Conference of the United Methodist Church in Arlington, Virginia.

ROBIN T. ADAMS is the rector of the Church of the Word (Anglican), Gainesville, Virginia.

TOM BERLIN is the lead pastor of Floris United Methodist Church, Herndon, Virginia.

RUSTY BROCK is the senior minister at First Baptist Church, Clemson, South Carolina.

JOHN PAUL CARTER is a retired pastoral counselor in Weatherford, Texas.

JOHN KILLINGER is a writer and retired pastor and professor living in Warrenton, Virginia.

CONTRIBUTORS

Rachel Lackey and Jim Strickland are the Co-directors of The Sabbath House in Bryson City, North Carolina.

Bill J. Leonard is the James and Marilyn Dunn Professor of Church History at Wake Forest University, Winston-Salem, North Carolina.

Benjamin Maas is the rector at St. James' Episcopal Church, Warrenton, Virginia.

J. Robert Moon is a former Baptist pastor and is currently an Episcopal layperson in Bull Run, Virginia.

Donna S. Mote is the Episcopal chaplain to the Hartsfield-Jackson Atlanta International Airport in Atlanta, Georgia.

Oliver Rooper is a retired Episcopal priest in Georgia.

Keith Savage is the senior servant at the First Baptist Church of Manassas in Manassas, Virginia.

Tim Shirley is the senior minister at the United Community Church of Sun City Center in Sun City Center, Florida.

Lou Snead is a retired Presbyterian minister in Austin, Texas.

Dallas Stallings is a retired Baptist pastor in Durham, North Carolina.

Michael Tassler is the pastor of Grace Lutheran Church in Colorado Springs, Colorado.

ACKNOWLEDGEMENTS

To the contributors of this collection of essays—Cathy Abbott, Robin Adams, Tom Berlin, Rusty Brock, John Paul Carter, Rachel Lackey, Bill Leonard, Donna Mote, Ben Maas, Oliver Rooper, Lou Snead, Keith Savage, Dallas Stallings, Jim Strickland, Michael Tassler, and Tim Shirley. Writing about wealth can be challenging, particularly for ministers. I am indebted to these colleagues who were willing to share their stories of success, failures, fears, and joys that they have experienced in the murkiness where wealth and ministry connect.

To my good friend, Dr. Daniel Kroger, Coordinator for Music and Liturgy at Holy Cross Catholic Church, Vero Beach, for his consistent encouragement to me. We push each other to explore the outer limits of practical theological education. Dan's help in editing my story and shaping the solicitation for contributors was essential.

To Dr. Eric Killinger, publisher and owner of The Intermundia Press, LLC, for his artistic and editorial hand in the production of this

ACKNOWLEDGEMENTS

collection, including the design of the cover art. His assistance in transferring these collections, typesetting and editing these various contributions into an attractive format made my task as editor so much easier.

To my partners, Mark G. Cooke and David K. Morton, at Heritage Financial, LLC, who supported my efforts with the financial backing for this production. To my co-workers, Elizabeth Clark and Jaqkee deBeauclair, who gave me space at my office to solicit the contributions and tolerated my almost daily excitement over the growing collection of essays. And specifically to Mark Cooke, for his vision to continue our focus on generosity and pastoral care by equipping ministers to serve the affluent in their congregations and communities. It was Mark's suggestion that I continue to move forward after the successful production of *My Pastor, My Money, and Why We're Not Talking* (2012) that pushed me to the next step.

To Dr. John Killinger, who helped me define the next step—an anthology of current opinions and attitudes toward wealth from the ministers who are our primary audience. John started the ball rolling by contributing the first essay I received. His willingness to be open about his journey was a source of encouragement for others to share their stories.

To my wife, Mariann Lynch, for her patience and encouragement in hearing my excitement about every step of progress tiny or large in this project.

ABOUT THE EDITOR

Robert Moon's familiarity with the tensions within pastoral care on the subject of wealth comes from his combined experience in ministry, poverty, pastoral care, and affluence. He served over twenty years as a senior pastor and grew up in inner city missions serving the homeless and destitute. He has also spent over ten years in not-for-profit administration and currently works in financial advisory and wealth management services.

Other publications by Robert include *My Pastor, My Money, and Why We're Not Talking: Bridging the Gap between the Pastor and Those With Wealth* (2012) and *Unemployment and How to Survive It* (2003). Additional white papers include "Three Major Challenges in Generosity and How to Overcome Them Through Donor Advised Funds"; "Enhancing Generosity in the Congregation Through Donor Advised Funds"; "Enhancing Generosity to Support Not For Profits Through Donor Advised Funds"; and "Pastoral Care in the Context of Sudden

ABOUT THE EDITOR

Wealth." Forthcoming publications include "All Saints Intersection" (2015), and "A Parable of Two Sons Revisited."

Robert received his bachelor of art degree in sociology from Georgia Southern University, Statesboro, Georgia. His seminary training includes a master of divinity degree from Southwestern Baptist Theological Seminary, Fort Worth, Texas, and a doctor of ministry degree from Southern Baptist Theological Seminary, Louisville, Kentucky. He also holds a master in business administration degree from the University of Colorado-Denver.

Robert is a partner in a wealth management firm in Northern Virginia where he resides with his wife, Mariann Lynch. He can be reached via email at jrobertmoon@gmail.com. For more information visit www.heritagefinllc.com, www.mypastormymoney.com, or LinkedIn.

CPSIA information can be obtained at www.ICGtesting.com
Printed in the USA
LVOW12s0341170115

423169LV00005B/10/P